LISA UNFRIED

Into the Dragon's Den

◉ LUCIDBOOKS

Into the Dragon's Den

Copyright © 2023 by Lisa Unfried

Published by Lucid Books in Houston, TX
www.LucidBooks.com

All rights reserved. No part of this publication may be reproduced, stored in a retrieval system, or transmitted in any form by any means, electronic, mechanical, photocopy, recording, or otherwise, without the prior permission of the publisher, except as provided for by USA copyright law.

ISBN: 978-1-63296-987-3
eISBN: 978-1-63296-626-1

Special Sales: Most Lucid Books titles are available in special quantity discounts. Custom imprinting or excerpting can also be done to fit special needs. Contact Lucid Books at Info@LucidBooks.com

Dedicated to my grandchildren.

MAY THE LIGHT WITHIN LEAD YOU TO ALL TRUTH.

Contents

Chapter 1: Why Me? 1
Chapter 2: A Stranger's Home 9
Chapter 3: Who am I? 15
Chapter 4: A Night of Dreams 23
Chapter 5: Again at Gigi's 30
Chapter 6: The Cave 40
Chapter 7: Jessica's Door 51
Chapter 8: A Strange World 57
Chapter 9: Nabuta 69
Chapter 10: Training Begins 78
Chapter 11: Jessica's Quest 89
Chapter 12: The Lost Base 101
Chapter 13: Caleb joins the Journey 113
Chapter 14: Discovery 125
Chapter 15: The Resonator Room 132
Chapter 16: The Assembly Room 137
Chapter 17: Freedom 143
Chapter 18: Too Late 146

Chapter 19: Sacrifice 155
Chapter 20: Judgment..166
Chapter 21: Rescue 174
Chapter 22: Onward 182
Acknowledgments 187

CHAPTER 1
Why Me?

Standing on the sidewalk, Daniel gazed at the narrow strip of uneven pavement alongside the street. Old homes, clipped lawns, and large, sweeping trees framed his neighborhood. Most would find this small-town vibe relaxing or peaceful. Daniel did not. His experience had been quite different. This morning, Daniel had taken too long to get ready for school and decided to take a different route, hoping to get there more quickly. He had not counted on running into Justin and his two goons.

Daniel watched the three teenage boys race away in the distance, periodically turning back to look at Daniel, pointing and laughing as they grew smaller and smaller. Daniel heard the faint sound of the school's buzzer in the distance. He would be late a third time. Principal Collins had warned him. "Three strikes, you're out!" Before the move, Daniel had never been late to school.

Being late again would mean a suspension and consequences

from his mother. Daniel could still hear her voice. "I'm sorry, Daniel. I know you didn't want to leave your home and your friends, but I can't do this on my own anymore. I had to come back home. I need help, and this is my last resort. Please, Honeybee, help me make this work for us." She had been so sincere and pleading that all Daniel could do was smile and nod.

Daniel's attention was now drawn to the cool liquid invading his once pristine socks and seeping onto his feet. He saw a thin layer of mud running across the sidewalk, the obvious source of the moisture. Now would be a great time for shoes. At his previous school—again, before the move—his socks and pants were never muddy. No one had ever noticed Daniel. Why should they?

Daniel stopped looking at his feet, lifted his head, and looked up at a pair of white Sketchers swaying gently on an electrical wire that stretched from a nearby house to the street. A large, dark shadow crossed the sky above his head. He searched the morning sky but found nothing that would create the shadow. His thoughts turned dark as he looked back at the swinging shoes. *Is it my fault Justin Collins hates me? Is it my fault he has two of the school's biggest football players as his best friends and bodyguards? Is it my fault I am more into books and video games than sports? Okay, that is probably true, but so what! Why does this keep happening to me? It's not my fault. Justin is the bad one here. I wish he would get what he has coming.*

If Daniel walked home now without his shoes, his mother would be upset. She didn't understand. She was always complaining about buying Daniel new clothes. She often declared that they didn't have money for his sudden growth spurts and that more clothes and shoes wouldn't help the situation.

This was the third time this month that Justin and his bullying friends had tried to mess with Daniel. Each time, they won. Today was no exception. Alex, perhaps the only friend Daniel had at the new school, was right. Daniel was just a doormat waiting for someone like Justin to wipe their feet on, but what could he do? He was just a kid who didn't want trouble. There had been enough trouble in his 14 years. Why was he still going through this? Why did he have to be the son of the small-town prodigal daughter? Unsure of his next move, Daniel looked again at the shoes dangling from the electrical line above him.

"They won't come down that way." The melodic voice startled Daniel.

"Huh?" answered Daniel, looking around to find the source of the comment.

"You can't stare them down," said the small, plump, elderly, gray-haired woman standing on the lawn near the porch of the nearby house. With her wrist, she brushed a gray tendril away from her face, trying to avoid a muddy garden glove. Daniel didn't know how long she had been standing there watching him. Then he noticed the garden hose in her hand and realized where the water and mud on the pavement had come from.

Daniel was unsure of what to do. "Don't mind your socks," she said in her childlike voice. "They're already dirty. Go to the side of the house, and bring the ladder that's there. We can get your shoes down with it. Everything will be all right. Come on, I need to get back to my gardening." Daniel followed the woman's pointing finger. He stared for only a moment, taking one last look down at his muddy socks. He shrugged his shoulders and bounded across the yard and around a huge purple hydrangea bush to retrieve the ladder. It would mean dirty socks, but they were already dirty and could be washed. He needed his shoes. Besides, he was only going to the side of the old house, not inside. What could happen?

The only ladder he could find was a metal A-frame leaning on its side against the brick. Daniel wasn't heavy on science, but he knew electricity and metal didn't mix. He wasn't sure what this old lady knew about any of that. Perhaps she had something rubber to shield him from the electricity in the wire. A science teacher had once told him, "You can protect yourself from electrical shock if you have something nonconductive such as rubber between you and the electricity." Daniel hoped the lady had thought of that.

Bringing the ladder across the yard, Daniel felt his feet slosh in the recently watered grass, another problem when dealing with electricity. He set up the ladder beneath his shoes that were still dangling on the wire running from the woman's house to the pole by the street. He started to climb the ladder to get his shoes, wondering if he would be able to pull the shoes down without touching the wire. But the ladder wasn't high enough.

He felt something tap his leg. "Get down here, sonny. Let

Why Me?   5

me do that." The woman was tapping him with a metal cane. Daniel had always been told to respect his elders, and she seemed determined. So he climbed back down the ladder and watched her climb to the top, holding her metal cane in one hand. When she reached the top of the ladder, Daniel realized that she was also too short to reach his shoes. He watched in horror as she lifted her metal cane to dislodge the dangling sneakers. The ladder shook slightly, but the woman steadied herself and then reached again with the cane for his shoes. Daniel wondered if the rubber tip on the cane would be enough to block the current of the electrical wire. He was wishing he had argued more with the woman and not let her take the lead in the rescue operation. The ladder swayed a bit more. Daniel started to reach for it but stopped when he thought it might be carrying an electrical current. At any moment he thought he might see sparks, hear the crackling of electricity, and smell the burning ozone and possibly the woman's flesh. He stood in horror, expecting the worst. "Open your eyes, sonny. I got your shoes," the woman said, looking down at Daniel.

Daniel looked up at his rescued shoes dangling from the woman's hand and then at the woman still teetering atop the ladder. As she lowered her cane, it touched the wire, and Daniel's heart leaped in his chest. What would he do? *If my mother would just let me have my own cell phone, I would be able to call 911. Should I run into the woman's home to use her phone? Would that be the right thing to do? Should I yell? Would anyone hear?*

"Sonny, what are you staring at?" The woman stood next

to him, brushing down her apron with one hand, his shoes in the other.

Daniel tilted his head to the side and questioned the woman. "How did you do that without getting electrocuted? I saw you touch the wire with your cane." Daniel stared at the woman in amazement.

The woman laughed and pointed at the wire. "Things are not always as they seem." Tracing the wire, Daniel noticed that it ran from the corner of her house to the pole at the street, and then to a second pole on the other side of the street where it ended. "There's no electricity in that wire. They cut the line when they installed a new wire in the ground." She shook her head, adding, "Can't get anybody to remove the old one."

Daniel smiled. "I see what you mean."

The woman turned to go back to her house. Then she stopped, looked back at Daniel, and asked, "How many times has Justin made you late?"

"This will be my third," Daniel replied and dropped his head.

"Principal Collins doesn't take kindly to kids being late to school. Please put the ladder back. I'll call Principal Collins and see what I can do for you." She smiled a gigantic smile and turned to head into the house. "Come to the porch when you are done."

Daniel shrugged his shoulders, folded the ladder, and then sloshed across the wet grass to return the ladder to the side of the house. Back at the front of the house, he sat on the steps to the front porch and pulled off his wet, dirty socks. He figured

Why Me?

he could brave the blisters and wear his shoes without socks. As he was about to put one foot in his shoe, he heard the woman on the phone with whom he assumed was Principal Collins. "Well now, Alicia, if you're going to let that boy intimidate others, you're going to have to stop picking on the loser. Yes, I know they need to learn to stand up for themselves. Why don't you let me try something? I need a little help around the house today. You can call it community service in lieu of suspension. I'm sure he'll be in school bright and early tomorrow morning. Yes, yes! I know. Thank you, Alicia. And don't forget. You promised to bring the family for dinner on Saturday. I'm looking forward to it. Bye-bye now."

The woman spoke to Daniel from behind the screen door. "Everyone calls me Gigi. I've got a fresh batch of cookies if you'd like one." Daniel jumped. How did she get to the door so fast?

Where Daniel previously lived, his response to the cookie invitation would have been an easy "No, thank you." Small towns were different, but crazy people did live in small towns too. Then Daniel caught the smell of fresh-baked cookies, lemon maybe, his favorite. He wasn't sure why he followed her inside, but something made him feel it would be all right. As he stepped just inside the house, he heard the lady call out, "Let's see if we can't get your socks clean. Do you like lemonade or milk with your cookies?"

Daniel hesitated, the screen door pressed on his backside, his shoes still in his hands. "I think maybe I should just go on to school, Ma'am." This was not something he was used to. In the city, you just don't go into strangers' homes. Something like this always happens in the first scene of a horror movie, and no one comes out alive. *What would my mom say if I never came home? Would Mom even know what happened?*

"It's Gigi! Remember?" Gigi spoke from the narrow hallway in front of Daniel. "Why are you still standing by the door? Come on in. And close the door behind you. It's all taken care of." The screen door creaked as Daniel let it finish closing behind him, but he decided to leave the wooden door open. Gigi appeared in the hallway again with a huge smile on her face. She walked past Daniel and closed the front door. Daniel stood frozen, just inside the door.

CHAPTER 2

A Stranger's Home

Gigi stopped next to Daniel and laughed. "I must watch too many horror movies," she said. "This is always how they start." Still laughing, she walked down the hallway toward the back of the house. Daniel listened as every floorboard seemed to creak with her steps. "Don't worry," she called back to Daniel. "This town is too small for that. Besides, if you come up missing, they'll know right where to look for you." He heard her melodic voice coming from the next room. "I have lemon cookies and chocolate ice cream," she sang back.

Daniel turned to look at the closed front door and then back toward the rear of the house. Cautiously walking down the little hallway, he heard the same creaks as he moved along its dimly lit passageway.

The hall opened to a bright kitchen. On a small table was a thick, green plate of thin, yellow wafers. Gigi stood at the counter nearby scooping ice cream. "I love chocolate and lemon together. They're my favorite."

Daniel smiled. They were his favorite too. "Can I call my mom and let her know where I am?" he asked.

Gigi paused for a moment, looking out the small window above the sink. "Let's not bother her at work. I'll take you home later, and we can tell her then. I'm sure everything will be all right." Gigi smiled, and Daniel couldn't help but return a grin.

Daniel sat at the table and ate a cookie as he watched Gigi make a bowl of ice cream for herself. As they finished their treat, Daniel put the dishes in Gigi's sink. Then Gigi went out the back door in the kitchen to a narrow, screened-in porch. She placed Daniel's socks and some soap in a washing machine and started it. Picking up a broom from the corner, she handed it to Daniel and asked him to sweep the small porch. "Daniel, come find me when you are done," she said. "I need to do some reorganizing in the storage closet at the top of the stairs. I would like you to help me move some boxes." Then she went back into the house.

Daniel quickly swept the porch and returned the broom to the corner where Gigi had picked it up. Inside the house, he walked to the stairs near the front door. Suddenly, he heard a loud crack! Daniel had forgotten about Gigi. "Gigi, are you all right?" he yelled as he raced up the stairs.

"Oh, I'm fine. I just forgot I can't do what I used to. Come, and help me move these boxes, okay?" Gigi was out of breath.

One by one, Daniel and Gigi transferred a lifetime of keepsakes. As they worked, Gigi stopped and picked up a small, rectangular box and held it gently. The faded paper covering the box was intact and appeared clean. The box's lid sat on it

A Stranger's Home

securely. "I had forgotten about this," Gigi said, resting her hand gently on the lid. She sat down on a chair just outside the closet. Daniel sat cross-legged on the floor next to her.

"What is it?" Daniel asked, hoping she would open it. *What if it held jewels?* he thought. *Maybe it held letters from an old boyfriend. Girls always liked that sort of thing. Or it could have leaves and dirt from her childhood? That would be sort of boring.* Daniel waited.

"This was my armor," she said very softly as she tenderly ran her hand across the paper on the lid.

Daniel's eyebrows furrowed. "Armor?" he questioned.

Gigi laughed. "Yes, armor. Every child of the King needs his or her armor to fight their battles for the good of the kingdom." Gigi carefully opened the box. Inside was a multicolored, braided length of cord; a butterfly scarf pin; a brass-colored ring; the wheel from an old pair of skates; and a headband with multicolored beads attached to it. Gigi lifted the cord out of the box and whispered, "My mother always said, 'A three-strand cord isn't easily broken.'" She returned the braided cord to the box and gently closed the lid. Then she set the box on her lap and stared straight ahead.

"Are you a princess? Is that why you can tell people what to do?" Daniel whispered.

"No," Gigi laughed softly. "I am a daughter of the King, but not of this world."

"What world are you from?" Daniel was beginning to rethink his stepping inside this lady's house. She was more than a little weird. "Are you like an alien from another planet?"

Gigi stopped and thought about what Daniel had said. "I suppose you can put it like that. But it's not [Gigi lifted her arm into the air] just 'out there.' It's around us too." Gigi drew a circle in the air with her hand. "Sort of . . . another dimension." Daniel looked at Gigi's simple expression and decided he should change the subject of their conversation.

"So what are we doing with the closet?" Maybe if they got back to work, he could finish soon. Then he could go home.

Gigi pointed to the closet. "I want to move the boxes out so I can set up a quiet space to study the book and maybe find a new portal."

Daniel looked past Gigi and into the hall closet. There against the wall was a small desk and chair. An open book sat on the table, and a little lamp sat next to the book. There were notes pinned to the wall above the desk and on other walls of the closet, but Daniel couldn't make out any of them. "It looks like you already have everything set up. Is it okay if I stack the boxes in the hall for now? I really need to get home. School's almost out." Daniel sat back on his heels. He figured he didn't need his socks at that point.

Gigi sat quietly for a moment. Then she slapped her hands on her knees and stood up like she was a young woman. "Yes, you straighten the boxes in the hall here, and I will check on your socks." With that, she walked down the stairs to the little porch. By the time Daniel came down to meet her, his socks were clean and fresh. She grabbed her purse and keys from a little table by the door and led Daniel outside.

Gigi told Daniel to get in her car, and she would drive him

A Stranger's Home

home. The ride to Daniel's house was short, and Gigi never once asked Daniel where he lived. When she stopped in his driveway, Daniel made sure he had all his things, climbed out of the car, and walked toward his house. He turned to face the car as Gigi hollered, "You can stop by anytime, Daniel! I enjoyed our visit." Gigi waved vigorously, smiling from ear to ear, and drove away.

As Daniel walked up the driveway to his house, he saw his mother standing in the doorway. "I didn't make it to school today," Daniel stated. He stared at his mother's feet. She had already put on her pink, fuzzy house shoes.

"I know. Principal Collins called me. I don't mind your helping Gigi, but I'd rather you didn't make a habit of it. She's . . ." His mother paused and looked down the street where Gigi had gone.

Daniel chuckled. "I know. She's a nut job. She had me help her make room for a desk in her closet so she could find the portal to another dimension." Daniel rolled his eyes and shook his head. Then with a smile, he said, "It's because she's a space alien." Daniel stepped up to the threshold of the door and looked down at his mother's five-foot-two-inch frame. She shook her head and looked up at Daniel's six-foot frame.

"Well, I wouldn't put it like that, but, well . . . I don't know. You are right. She's different." Daniel's mother sighed.

"That's okay, Mom. I'm not planning to go back." Daniel looked again at his mother's pink slippers. "You have a rough day today?" Not waiting for an answer, he squeezed past his mom in the doorway and headed up the stairs to his room.

"We'll talk more about this later, okay?" his mom called behind him.

"Sure, Mom. Later." Daniel went to his room and shut the door. He flipped on his computer and clicked on the link to his favorite game. He slashed his sword through vines and began his quest in search of the glittery dragon. Suddenly, a wizard appeared on the lower right corner of the video screen. "Wait! Where is your armor? Here. Take this." In the wizard's hand was an old, paper-covered box like Gigi's. Daniel froze as he looked at the box. He sat back and abruptly turned the computer game off.

"Daniel," his mother called, "dinner is ready." Daniel sat at the table and stared at the stew his mother had placed in front of him on the table. When he finished the bowl of stew, his mother placed a second bowl on the table in front of him.

Daniel stared at the second bowl of soup. "Uh, Mom, I think I've had enough for dinner tonight." Looking up at his mom, he smiled and added, "It was great." Daniel's mom casually picked up the bowl and dumped the contents back into the soup pot. She then turned and left the kitchen, looking more tired than before.

Daniel left the table and returned to his room to play more video games. He stared at the monitor for a moment and then turned it off and climbed into bed. *I'll think about it tomorrow*, he told himself and rolled over, closing his eyes.

CHAPTER 3

Who am I?

Daniel stood in front of the wall of metal lockers. One more class period, and he would go back to his little sanctuary for the entire weekend. Only three more weeks and it would be summer break with the hope of escaping the torment of school. Daniel faced his locker. The combination lock worked easily. *Thank you for whatever brought good luck for that.* Down the hall he could hear another student banging their locker to force it open.

Daniel held his books in the crook of his left arm. His right arm reached inside the open locker. His hand had just touched his science book when he heard someone behind him.

Please go away, please go away, please go away. It repeatedly ran through his brain. Suddenly, his shoulders slammed into the front of the locker. His sandy-red hair swept into his face as his head hit the top edge. Bruises from an earlier altercation cried out, but Daniel remained silent. He didn't want to turn around. He knew Justin and his goons were behind him.

"Hey, Danny, can't get your head out of your locker?" Justin taunted. Timothy Garza and Alonzo Guerra stood snickering behind Justin. Daniel turned around to face his mockers. The boys were dressed in army fatigue pants and white T-shirts that proclaimed, "Peace Church Youth Camp."

Justin ran his hand through long shocks of blonde hair that were hanging in his face, framed by shaved sides. Justin wiped his nose with his thumb and then pushed Daniel back against his locker. Daniel hit the back of his head on his locker, which caused him to see stars. Justin and his gang turned and walked away, laughing. "Looks like you're going to be late for class again, Danny Boy," Justin called back over his shoulder. Daniel watched the three bullies strut away.

The walls and rows of lockers started to fade, and Daniel felt himself sliding down. He managed to catch himself a foot or so above the floor. Through the stars, he could hear his mother. "Sweetie, I know this isn't the best thing, but I haven't done well since we've been on our own, and coming home was the only way I could make it. Things will get better. I promise." He felt her hand on top of his left shoulder.

As the stars faded along with the image of his mother, he realized that the hand on his shoulder belonged to Miss Lattimore. Her classroom door was close to Daniel's locker. He wondered how much she had heard or if it even mattered.

Miss Lattimore tried to help Daniel lift his six-foot frame upward along the wall. At five foot four inches, she found it difficult. "I'm sorry. I should have come out of my classroom sooner. This is my off period. Let's get you to the nurse's office." She looked down the hall toward the main corridor, her lips tight and her brown curls shaking as she spoke. "I want to let Principal Collins know what happened." Over the sound of the bell, Daniel heard Miss Lattimore ask if he was able to walk. Daniel nodded.

"I'm okay," he said. "I think I can make it to class now." Miss Lattimore helped Daniel stand on his own.

"Come on, Daniel. I want you to get checked out by the school nurse." Miss Lattimore looked up at him, her hands on her hips and feet planted solidly on the floor. The glare in her brown eyes told Daniel that she was not going to give him a choice. He stepped toward the middle of the hallway with Miss Lattimore following him, reaching up to gently rest her hand on his shoulder. When they reached the end of the hall, she steered him in the opposite direction from his class and toward the nurse's office.

When they arrived at the nurse's office, Miss Lattimore opened the door and directed Daniel to sit down inside. Then she closed the door and stepped across the hall to Principal Collins' door. Quietly she knocked. "Come in," called Principal Alicia Collins, and Miss Lattimore went inside. It was a small office. The principal sat behind a large desk covered in papers. Two plain wooden chairs were in front of her desk. There was one narrow bookshelf with scattered books along one wall. The top of the bookshelf was covered with various objects, including a waving cat, a fat Buddha, and two dragons of different sizes and styles. Principal Collins let out a slow breath. "What can I do for you today, Miss Lattimore?"

Staring at the Indian dream catcher hanging behind Principal Collins' desk, Jazmine Lattimore replied, "Justin has been at it again terrorizing other students." Principal Collins blinked and turned her gaze to the woman standing in front of her. Miss Lattimore continued. "Justin was in the hall with his friends and slammed another student into his locker. You cannot keep letting your son get away with this. Someone is going to get hurt."

Principal Collins looked around the room as though searching for support. Jazmine Lattimore didn't miss the glance. "Miss Lattimore, boys will be boys," the principal said. "The roughhousing will lead them to learn to fight for themselves later in life."

"The student they accosted was Daniel Pierce. I believe you know who he is. You're not going to do anything about it, are you?" Miss Lattimore wasn't afraid to snap back at Principal Collins.

The principal glanced around the office.

"And by the way," Miss Lattimore continued. "Are we now allowing religious artifacts in this school? I thought such things were banned here."

"No! Of course not," Principal Collins spat back.

"Well, then, why do you have a dream catcher, a Native American artifact, a Buddha statue, a picture of a creature with a third eye, and dragons around your office?" Miss Lattimore couldn't seem to control herself.

Principal Collins suddenly stood up behind her desk. "I'm allowed to display art objects from my travels abroad, Miss

Who am I?

Lattimore. Do you like your job? Would you like to keep it? I suggest you stick to language and the arts. This matter is closed! Good day!"

Jazmine Lattimore stood for a moment with her mouth open and then closed it quickly and spun around. She walked to the door of the principal's office, opened it, and walked out, closing it swiftly behind her.

Once outside, she came face to face with Daniel. She drew in a deep breath, let it out slowly, and addressed Daniel in a much calmer voice. "Daniel, what did the nurse say?"

"She said I was fine and to return to class," Daniel replied.

"Please go to your next class. Stop by the secretary's desk, and she will give you a pass." Miss Lattimore turned and left the school administration office. Daniel stood a moment before heading to the secretary's desk.

When Daniel had walked into the nurse's office, no one was there, so he sat in a chair outside Principal Collins' office and listened to the conversation going on behind the closed door. Daniel stopped by the secretary's desk, picked up the pass, and left the school administration office just as the bell rang for the end of the day. *Who am I?* Daniel thought.

In the hall, Mr. Hawthorn, Daniel's science teacher, stopped and placed his hand heavily on Daniel's shoulder. Daniel flinched. "Daniel, we missed you in class this afternoon." Daniel showed him the pass. "I figured as much," his teacher said. "You know, Daniel, you are going to have to learn to stand up to Justin and his friends. Life doesn't bring imaginary people to rush in and help you. Just don't stop standing." Mr. Hawthorn patted Daniel's shoulder where it had hit the side of his locker, and Daniel almost slumped to the floor. Mr. Hawthorn didn't seem to notice but repeated, "Keep standing." Mr. Hawthorn turned and walked out the main doors of the school building.

Daniel was still standing just inside the main doorway, pausing before exiting the school when Alex Rodriquez punched him playfully in the arm. Daniel flinched again. "Hey, man," Alex said. "Missed you in science class. What happened?" Daniel turned to face Alex, who added, "Justin at it again? Wow! What did he do to your head? Are you okay?"

Daniel sighed. "Yeah. Just spent the last period in the nurse's office."

Alex nodded and continued. "What is with that kid? I guess you can get away with anything if your mom is the principal." Daniel nodded in agreement. Alex continued. "Got any plans for this weekend? I'm sleepin' in. I'm ready for some real down time." Alex smiled at Daniel.

Daniel touched the knot on his forehead, flinching at the unrealized pain. *I'm all right.* He remembered his mother's words—*Everything will be all right.* Daniel thought to himself. *Yeah, this week is going so great, really!*

Daniel nodded in agreement. "Yeah, real down time." Both boys chuckled.

Jessica Truman brushed past Daniel and Alex and stepped outside. If she was quick, she might be able to get away before Eric showed up.

"Hey, Babe! Let me give you a ride home. You know I live right next door. It would be so easy," Eric, a senior, hollered from the sidewalk in front of the school. He had been leaning against his new, red convertible.

"I'm sorry, Eric." Jessica yelled back. "Not today. I need to talk to someone." Jessica turned around, reentered the school, and ran into Daniel. Giving Daniel a quick glance, she stepped around him and went farther into the school building.

Jessica headed down the hallway going anywhere. *Why does a senior care about a first-year student? He's just looking for a new conquest. Well, it won't be me.* At that moment, Jessica collided with Samantha Harris. "Excuse me," Jessica muttered, turning to face Samantha momentarily.

"Excuse you, indeed!" Samantha stopped, spinning around to face Jessica. "How rude!" Samantha pushed Jessica's shoulder, but Jessica kept going down the hallway. "You have always thought of yourself as better than the rest of us," Samantha yelled. Jessica ignored her. Samantha, who was with three of her friends, twirled around and headed out the school doors. Just outside, Samantha spotted Eric.

The girls waved enthusiastically. "Eric! Oh, Eric! Is that your new car? Can we have a ride?"

Eric grinned, opening the door for them.

Daniel and Alex continued to stand in the school doorway and watch the scene. Eric held the car door open for the girls. Justin and his buddies were still outside and had just pulled a heavy backpack off a fellow student's shoulders. The kid stumbled around as the boys tried to grab the bag. Then they ran down the sidewalk, laughing and pointing at their mischief. A dark, angular cloud cast a shadow over the scene.

Suddenly, Daniel noticed Jessica standing next to them. Alex broke the silence. "Don't you wish you could just wave a wand and make bad things happen to them? Not really bad, just something where they would get a taste of their own medicine."

Daniel thought for a moment.

Jessica responded. "Be careful what you wish for."

Daniel added, "No, I don't wish that. Then we'd be just like them. What would that do?"

"Yeah," Alex replied. "I guess you're right."

The three stepped out the school doors, and each one went their own way home.

CHAPTER 4

A Night of Dreams

Daniel opened his eyes slowly. Sand stung his face and arms. He rubbed his eyes but felt no pain from the sand in them. The sandstorm continued to beat against him softly. *How did I get here? Is this a dream? It feels very real.* He looked around but could see nothing in the swirling sand. In the distance, a form slowly began to take shape. He watched it begin to grow taller as it walked toward him. It took the shape of a man and then slowly morphed into his father dressed in sand-colored, military, camouflage fatigues. The storm seemed to disappear as a bubble formed around them. Now Daniel knew this was a dream. His father had been one of many soldiers who had not come home from the war.

Daniel's dad squatted down and hugged his son. "I miss you so much, Bumble Bee." His father held him for what felt like an eternity before releasing him. It had been a long time since Daniel had seen his dad, and he didn't want the moment to end. "I wanted to see you again so desperately," his dad said. "I don't have much time. Do you remember how I told you I wanted to protect my family and country? I know I haven't been there for you, but I have always loved you. I've always understood there was a bigger battle between good and evil. Now the King has asked me to join a bigger fight, one to protect everyone from an even greater evil. I will be going even farther away, but I will never be far from you. I will be able to watch over you better, and I will be there anytime you need me."

Daniel's dad gave him another long, tight hug. Then he leaned back and pulled what looked like a familiar box from behind his back. "This is something my mother helped me put together when I was a little younger than you. I have kept it with me always. I hoped I could help you create your own, but since I won't need mine anymore, I want this to be yours. Hold onto it with all you have in you." Daniel's dad carefully lifted the old, worn, tattered box lid. Daniel looked in the box and noted items that seemed rather unimpressive. As he lifted his hand to reach inside, his dad closed the lid. Daniel couldn't remember why the box looked familiar.

"You must wait until I am gone before you look through the box. Please, don't lose it. Someday you will understand what each piece means. In the meantime, this is very important. Do this for me, please. I love you, Bumble Bee." His dad stood up and looked down at Daniel. "I am heading off to fight for the King. Remember me, and know that I will love you always." His dad stepped back and saluted his son.

A Night of Dreams

"I'll remember, Dad," Daniel whispered as he stood as tall as he could and returned his father's salute.

Daniel awoke—no sand, no wind, just the sound of gentle snoring from the Malamute on the floor near his bed. The dream had ended. He sat up and looked around him. Shadows stretched across the floor and walls, running away from the soft glow on the carpet from a night light on the far wall. His room looked the same—mattress strewn with blankets and quilts, a simple chest of drawers under a window on the far wall, and his small desk along the wall next to the door. It looked the same as it did every night. A tear ran down Daniel's cheek. He quickly brushed it away.

He lay back down and closed his eyes, trying to remember the first time he had the dream. He had woken up from that dream to the sound of his mother's cell phone. "Hello, this is Laura," she mumbled softly as a garbled voice spoke on the other end. After a moment, the phone went silent. Daniel had opened his door just enough to watch his mother. She stood in the hallway staring at nothing. Then abruptly she threw the phone down the hall to the farthest wall, breaking it. "I knew you would do this to me!" She screamed as though Daniel's father, Cody, could hear her a million miles away. She turned, went into her bedroom, and slammed the door behind her. Daniel had heard his mother crying softly.

The next day, two men in military uniforms came to the house with a folded flag that they presented to his mother. When they left, she dropped the flag in the trash by the door and went to the kitchen.

Daniel's memory was fading now as he heard the hall clock chime four times. He lay back on his bed and continued thinking. Even at the age of six, he would never forget that day.

His dad had left for the military when Daniel was only two. His parents divorced shortly after that. While Daniel was unable to see his father in person, they spoke often by video call. When his dad was on leave and in town, Daniel saw him for weeks at a time. Immediately after his father's death, Daniel asked his mother about his dad. However, over time it seemed to upset her, so Daniel stopped asking.

Now, what seemed like only a moment later, Daniel woke to the insistent barking of Angel, his Malamute. He reached down to silence the dog and inadvertently fell out of bed. Where was that dog? Daniel looked across his bedroom floor for Angel. Finally, he looked under the bed. There was Angel, guarding a small paper-covered box. Daniel tried to think how it could have gotten there. His brain grew foggy, and another vision filled his brain.

Was he still dreaming? Or was it a memory drifting across Daniel's brain? A little boy stood in a hallway holding a small cardboard box. "What have you got there?" his mother, Laura, asked her young son. She reached forward and took the box from Daniel's little hands. She stopped and stared at the box quizzically and then slowly and gently opened it. Tears began to well up in her eyes as she fingered the contents of the small box. She gently closed it and placed her hand on top. "These are things that were your dad's when he was younger. He started collecting the contents with his mom when he was a

A Night of Dreams

little older than you. Let me put this away for you until you are old enough." Laura held the box gently. Then she leaned over, kissed her son, and took the treasures with her to her room.

Daniel's mom seemed to struggle more and more with the everyday trials of life. When she announced they were moving, Daniel thought things would be better, but once again, they weren't.

The small alarm clock began vibrating on the floor next to Daniel's bed, and he realized that he had been dreaming all along. Daniel forced himself awake, rolled out of bed and onto the floor where he began searching for clean clothes for school. Then he remembered it was Saturday. That meant he could slip on his pants from the day before and put on a clean T-shirt. Socks wouldn't be necessary. After a quick trip to the bathroom, he was ready to enjoy his free time. He knew that at some point, his mom would give him a list of chores, and his free time would be over. For now, the time was his.

On his way to the bathroom, Daniel stopped when he thought he heard his mother on the phone. Her tone was stressed. "Yes, I know, Gigi."

Laura paused to let Gigi talk. "Of course, but you scared him with all your alien talk. He came home telling me he thought you were crazy, and he doesn't want to go back over there. Geez, you talk about the King so much. It's a wonder the town hasn't locked you up."

Laura paused again for Gigi's response. "Right. Okay."

Laura hung up the phone. Daniel continued to the bathroom and then returned to his room. His life was getting strange.

Daniel had received an old desktop computer from one of his mother's friends in the city just before they left. That gave him an escape through video games when he was not at school or doing his chores. He had placed the computer and monitor on the floor next to the wall, leaving his small desk for homework. He sat on the floor, leaned against his bed, turned on the computer, and reached for the controller. As he opened his favorite game, he waited for the strange wizard to reappear, but there was no wizard. As he was playing, he began to hear muffled voices downstairs. His mother's voice seemed tense, but he couldn't make out the second voice.

"Daniel!" His mother's voice echoed up the stairs. "Are you up yet? I need you downstairs, please." Slowly, Daniel paused his game and laid the controller next to him. Usually, his mother gave him more time than this. He reluctantly got up and made his way downstairs to see what she wanted. At the bottom of the stairs stood Gigi. Daniel hesitated before reaching the last step.

Gigi smiled and tilted her head slightly, looking at Daniel. Laura spoke first. "Daniel, Ms. Gigi has asked that you come back to her house so you two can finish the project you started the day you missed school. I have agreed to this." Daniel's forehead wrinkled. His mother continued. "Also, Ms. Gigi has promised to pay you for your time there. How do you feel about helping her out?" Daniel hesitated and looked out the glass door behind Gigi and his mom. He thought about the

A Night of Dreams

box in Gigi's closet. *Perhaps I'll get a chance to ask her more about it.*

Gigi continued to smile back at Daniel. After a few moments, she stopped smiling, turned to Laura, threw up her hands, and said, "If he doesn't want to, it's okay." She dropped her hands and turned to leave through the door behind her.

"No, wait!" Daniel shouted. Gigi stopped and turned to face the stairs and Daniel. "I'll help," he said. "I didn't mean to leave you with all those boxes in your hallway." Daniel tried to offer a sheepish grin to appease Gigi and his mom, who seemed upset that Daniel was hesitating to help.

Gigi clapped her hands in response, and the smile returned to her face. "Well, then, I will see you in about an hour," she said. "Bye now." She left the house with a single wave of her hand.

Daniel looked at his mom.

"Are you sure, Babe?" his mom asked. "You really don't have to if you don't want to." She gave Daniel a sort of half-smile, still hoping he would do the right thing because he wanted to.

"No, really, Mom. I'm okay with it, and it would be the right thing to do. Don't you always say to do the right thing?" Daniel smiled, raised one eyebrow, and tilted his head as he stared at his mother at the bottom of the stairs. She returned his smile, and Daniel swung around and grabbed the handrail, pulling himself to the next step and up the stairs. *Thirty minutes to play my video games, and then I will head over to Gigi's house. Maybe she will have another fresh batch of cookies.*

Forty-five minutes later, Daniel stepped out of his house and headed to Gigi's.

CHAPTER 5

Again at Gigi's

Daniel hesitated at Gigi's screen door. The wooden front door was open. He smelled a fresh batch of cookies. Questions ran through his head. *Hey, Gigi, where'd you get that box I saw the other day? Do you still have that box from the other day? Can I see it?*

"Daniel, come on in. I've got a fresh batch of chocolate chip cookies. Do you like those? I'm really glad you decided to come back and help me with the boxes. I don't know what I was thinking leaving them in the hall." Gigi was dressed in a bright yellow jumpsuit and a floral apron. Her smile brightened the room almost as much as the lights did.

Daniel returned the smile, opened the screen door, and stepped inside. He nodded toward the stairs. "Should I get started on the boxes in the hall? Where do you want me to put them?"

"Yes, yes, yes!" Gigi replied. "Let's get those boxes into the garage for now. I can start going through them and maybe get rid of some stuff. I've collected so much junk. I think it's time to clean house, don't you?" Gigi had her hand in the air making circles above her head like that was supposed to explain everything. She then turned to head back to the kitchen and her cookies. "Cookies are almost done," she called back.

Daniel wasn't sure what she was trying to show with the motion above her head. However, he decided he needed to continue moving boxes if he was going to get her to answer his questions. One by one, he moved the boxes to Gigi's garage and stacked them neatly in a corner. He finally moved the last box but saw no sign of the small box.

Daniel stopped in the kitchen for the cookies Gigi had promised. Sitting at the table, Daniel waited for Gigi to finish scooping two bowls of vanilla ice cream, which she topped with chocolate syrup, whipped cream, and chocolate chip cookies. Neither Daniel nor Gigi spoke.

When Daniel finished his cookies and ice cream, he placed his spoon in the empty bowl, took a deep breath, and said, "Gigi, I was wondering about the box you showed me."

"Which one, sweetie?" she replied as though she didn't know, though Daniel was sure she did.

"The small, paper-covered box," Daniel answered.

"Oh, that one. Well . . ." Gigi started. Then they heard the screen door squeak.

"Gigi? You around?" The voice rang through the house. Daniel recognized it—it was Miss Lattimore, his language arts teacher. When she joined them in the kitchen, she said, "I was planning to start a study of the writers of the Western

Mediterranean Sea and was hoping I could borrow some of your souvenirs from your travels there." Miss Lattimore glanced at Daniel. "Hi, Daniel! Say, Gigi, can I have some cookies and ice cream? You know chocolate chip is my favorite. Oh, and I love vanilla ice cream sundaes too." Jasmine Lattimore turned to the kitchen counter and grabbed a bowl, dipping herself some ice cream.

"Of course, you can," chuckled Gigi who barely looked up from her own bowl. "I was wondering if you would be stopping by. I heard about your discussion with Principal Collins yesterday."

Daniel remained confused about that conversation. He had heard what was said but didn't get the part about souvenirs or literature. Some adults had strange conversations.

Miss Lattimore sat at the table with Daniel and Gigi and began eating her ice cream and cookies. *I'm never going to find out about the box,* Daniel sighed to himself.

After Miss Lattimore had eaten most of her cookies and ice cream, she asked Gigi, "Are you going to bring up any of the issues tomorrow that we talked about last week at the school board meeting?" Then she shoved a spoonful of ice cream into her mouth.

Gigi sighed. "As the chairman of the school board, I will bring up the subject, but I can't make them vote the way I want them to. We will have to wait and see what the others think." With that, Gigi got up and took her bowl and placed it gently in the sink. Miss Lattimore stood, picked up her bowl, and placed it carefully in the sink as well.

Again at Gigi's

"Okay, Gigi," Miss Lattimore said. "I know you want what is best for the school and for the kids. I'll leave it to your wise words to address the matter." With that, she kissed Gigi on the cheek, waved at Daniel, and walked out of the house.

Gigi stood at the sink and sighed, and then turned to Daniel and smiled. Daniel stood to bring her his bowl, but Gigi waved for him to be seated and walked to the table to pick it up and set it in the sink herself.

Daniel sat back down and waited. Gigi shook her finger at Daniel. "I know what box you were asking about. You wait right here for just a minute." Then Gigi left the kitchen and headed to the front of the house. When she returned, she held the small box in her hands. She carefully placed it on the table in front of Daniel. "Now what do you want to know about this box?" she said as she sat down at the table near Daniel.

"Well, what is in the box? What is it for? And where is this other dimension you talked about?" Daniel asked, placing his elbows and then his hands on the table.

Gigi took a deep breath. "That's a lot of questions, but I understand what you are asking. Let me see if I can make some sense of it. Then you can decide what you choose to believe. Remember, what you believe in your heart will write the story of your life." Gigi patted Daniel's hand.

Gigi paused as though she was trying to decide if Daniel understood what she was saying. Then she sighed and continued. "We live in a battle of espionage and warfare every day. It's all around us. The battle is not just out there in the cosmos." Gigi pointed skyward.

"Like space aliens," interrupted Daniel.

"Well, if that helps you make sense of it, sure." Gigi smiled and continued. "But it's here on this planet too. In fact, our world is the center of the battle. We have been protected from this war because we are separated from it by a dimensional veil. Daniel, we are part of a greater kingdom—a kingdom that reaches to the farthest corners of the universe. This dimension or world of the King is all around us. We just can't see it. But if we try, we can feel it. It's more real than this one. But as time advances to its end, the veil between the two worlds is growing thinner."

Daniel noticed a plaque on the wall above the table.

....

We don't fight against our fellow man.
We fight against the Darkness,
against the evil forces of Wickedness not of this world.

....

Daniel pointed to the sign on the wall and asked, "So how do we fight this darkness, and what does this box have to do with it?"

Gigi placed her hand on the box. "This box holds the armor of a child of the King. The King is the one who rules all the realms."

Daniel thought for a minute. "Does he rule this realm too?"

"No, Daniel, we do. The King gave it to us. It is our responsibility, but many who have the authority don't know it or don't want to know about it. And another has been given control."

"The Darkness?" Daniel questioned. Though Daniel was deep in thought, Gigi could tell he didn't get it. "This is really hard to believe," Daniel said as he shook his head and snorted lightly.

"Many don't," Gigi replied. "That's why Darkness rules everywhere, except for places where the people believe the truth and have retaken their authority. Those who don't believe have given their ruling authority to the Darkness."

"And this armor makes you believe?" Daniel asked.

"No, the armor helps you fight your battles against the Darkness. It protects you," Gigi answered. "Would you like to see?" Gigi smiled and began opening the box on the table.

Not knowing what to expect, Daniel leaned forward to get a better look inside. He didn't expect the simple items the box held.

Gigi pulled out a multicolored cord. "This is my Belt of Truth."

"So like Wonder Woman's Lasso of Truth?" Daniel asked. "You hit someone with it, and they have to tell you the truth?"

Gigi giggled. "No, not like that. You have to understand that items from this realm do not work in the other realm. Sometimes weapons from the other realm will work here, but it takes great training for that to happen. I don't have the training for it myself, but there are those who can make things happen. Some of them work for the Darkness, though, so you must learn to know the difference." Gigi paused, and a frown crossed her face and then faded.

"No," Gigi continued, "this belt is something you wear to remind you of the truth of this world and the other. Then there is the Breastplate."

Daniel looked at the butterfly pin Gigi removed from the box. "That doesn't look like something I would wear," he added.

Gigi laughed. "Of course not. This is mine. My mother gave me this broach many years ago. It was her mother's. It reminds me that I am right in believing in the King, and he protects my heart from wrong. Then there are these skate wheels. They aren't really shoes, but they stand for Shoes of Peace. They tell me to always walk in peace toward others—or skate, if you like."

"That can be hard when others don't want to walk in peace with you," Daniel added under his breath.

"True, but that shouldn't stop you from trying," Gigi answered. When Daniel looked up, Gigi was smiling back at him. Daniel looked back at the box and pulled out a small ring.

"What's this for?" he asked.

"Oh, that's my Shield," Gigi answered. "It protected me from the jabs of the enemy. I would pretend that it expanded to whatever size I needed. The last thing in the box is my Helmet. It is really only a headband, but I would pretend it could extend to cover whatever part of my head that needed to be protected. In all this, I could hear the King tell me how important I was to him and how much he loved me."

Again at Gigi's

Daniel sat quietly as Gigi's mind seemed to wander. Daniel finally spoke to break the silence. "All that in that little box?" Daniel looked at the contents scattered on the table.

Gigi began to replace the contents. "I know. It's rather difficult to believe that any of this could be real, but maybe someday the King will show you who you really are."

"Wait!" Daniel suddenly stopped Gigi. "I overheard Miss Lattimore ask Principal Collins if she knew who I was. Who am I really?"

Gigi laughed. "It isn't as simple as that. But there is something I would like to tell you about your parents. You may have known that both your mother and your father came from this town. They met here and married before your father left for the Marines." Gigi paused. "But I need to discuss this with your mother before I go any further. It is more important that you know you are important to the King." Again, Gigi paused. "Why don't you take the box back upstairs and place it on the desk in the closet. I want to go through it again later. Can you do that for me, please?"

Gigi reached over and patted Daniel's arm. Then she placed her arms on the table in front of her. Looking at the table, she added, "I'm feeling a little tired right now. You'll find a little money on the desk. Thank you for helping me." Gigi looked back at Daniel. "Feel free to take the money, and head on home. I'm going to rest a bit." As Daniel reached for the small box of trinkets, Gigi patted his arm again and added, "Thank you for helping an old woman remember." Gigi smiled and placed her hands back on the table in front of her.

Daniel stood up and stopped for a minute, watching Gigi. Her smile had faded. It was the first time she looked very old to Daniel. "Are you going to be all right?" Daniel asked.

"Yes," Gigi replied, "I'm fine, just a little tired. I need to rest for a minute. You go on. Don't worry about me." Gigi smiled a weak smile at Daniel, and he slowly turned to the hallway and headed up the stairs.

At the top of the stairs, he entered the closet and set the box on the little table. It was the first time he had been able to see some of the words taped to the walls of the little closet. He slowly looked at the walls until several words caught his eye.

••

> *The only authority evil has over you is what you surrender to it.*

••
••

> *You must understand, I have imparted to you all my authority to trample over his kingdom. You will trample upon every evil one before you and overcome every power they have. Absolutely nothing will be able to harm you as you walk in my authority.*

••
••

> *The Spirit of Truth will come upon you, and you will be filled with power.*

••

Again at Gigi's

Daniel leaned over a box that was still on the floor and placed his hand against the back wall of the closet. He didn't remember leaving that box here but was careful not to disturb it. He wanted to read one last message.

··

We can ask the King to show us how evil is working against us or our family, and he will show us truth.

··

Daniel thought to himself, *I wish someone would show me the truth. This stuff just doesn't make sense to me. I wish I knew what I have to do with all this. It's crazy.* Suddenly, Daniel's hand that was supporting him against the back wall of the closet gave way (or should I say the wall gave way), and Daniel began to fall. Lights began flashing different colors all around him, and then everything went black.

CHAPTER 6

The Cave

Daniel felt something scurry across his face and swiped at it. Rising quickly, he hit his head on the ceiling above him and lay back down. "Ouch!" He rubbed his head trying to remember where he was. Opening his eyes revealed total darkness. Reaching with his hands, he found himself tucked in an alcove of rock and mud. Bugs and insects crawled everywhere. He quickly yet carefully rolled to his side to see if he could get out of this small space.

Just outside of the alcove, a tunnel ran in each direction with many other alcoves dug into its sides. A narrow vein ran through the rock walls of the tunnel, emitting a faint light. Carefully swinging his feet off the edge of the alcove, Daniel leaned forward so he wouldn't hit his head again. Looking down, he found the ground only a couple of feet below. He slid out of the alcove and dropped onto the floor of the roughly hewn tunnel. It was damp, warm, and soft with mud.

The Cave

The faint glowing vein allowed him to see a short distance down the tunnel in both directions. Daniel tried desperately to remember how he got here and where he had been the day before. What was he doing that could have caused him to end up in such a filthy place? All he wanted was to go home, but he didn't know where home was. Looking right and left, he couldn't see very far down the tunnel. A rat ran across his foot and down the hall. Something reached out from another alcove and grabbed the rat. Crunching sounds followed. Shivers ran down Daniel's spine.

He began to realize that he, too, was hungry. He needed to get out of there. He needed to find food, and he was not wrapped in the hope that there might be a kitchen somewhere.

Daniel decided to move down the hall away from the rat-eater, hoping this was the right direction. As he walked, he found other alcoves. Many of them held creatures he was not familiar with. Some creatures had fur, some had leathery skin, and others had the same soft skin that he had. Many were asleep, and those who were not looked more than a bit frightening with contorted faces and misshapen features. The creatures seemed unaware of him. If he tried to get their attention, they often reached out and tried to grab him, which required him to fight them off. One looked like an alligator with human arms, and one reminded him of a wolf except it looked like it had not eaten for a very long time. The skin around its face was sunken, its eyes protruded, and its lips pulled back from its teeth, which seemed too large for its mouth. The fur was matted and muddy. Its tongue hung out of its mouth to one side, and its eyes were glassy. Daniel avoided the wolf-like creature. He decided to avoid all the creatures.

After some time, Daniel became tired. The walls and ceiling seemed to be getting smaller. The openings and the hallway seemed to be shrinking, and the air was definitely growing hotter. The glowing minerals he had seen were diminishing. Daniel questioned if he had gone in the right direction. He was frightened and confused. He stopped for a moment and looked behind him. A lizard crawled across the floor and ran away. He could swear the lizard had muttered something ugly to him, but he wasn't aware of a talking lizard. He continued to walk and push forward. He fought the fatigue in his legs and the fog in his brain.

Was he asleep? Was he dreaming? What was going on?

When Daniel felt he could go no farther, he found another alcove. He looked and then reached inside. When he found it was empty, he crawled up into it. *Is this how I got into this place? Why am I here? Where is my mom? Where is my life?* Just as he began to doze off, something pushed him out onto the ground. He felt something else pounce on top of him. *Is this the wolf, the alligator, or another one of the creatures?* He started beating and kicking his assailant. He finally rose and ran back the other way, down the long corridor. He wasn't sure if the creature was after him, but he had to get away. He had obviously gone the wrong way. Daniel was tired, but he knew he couldn't stay there. He had to find help.

When Daniel thought he was far enough away, he stopped and listened. All he could hear was his own heavy breathing.

The Cave

His legs ached, and he was tired. *Where is my mom?* He leaned against the wall to catch his breath and slid down, trying to remember his family, trying to remember what it was that he knew about them. He closed his eyes and began to cry. Big boys weren't supposed to cry. Then he felt something heavy strike the side of his head and fell to his side. Something grabbed his foot, and he could feel himself being dragged. Then everything went black.

"Bumble Bee, where are you? Come on, Bumble Bee. Stop hiding. Where are you?" The sweet song-like words drifted into Daniel's ears. "There you are." Daniel felt himself being picked up and swung around. "Come and play with me. I love you, Bumble Bee!" Daniel opened his eyes. A handsome, young man had picked him up and placed him on his hip. They were facing a large mirror. "Hey, Bumble Bee, can you see yourself here?"

Daniel saw himself in a mirror, in the arms of the handsome, young man. Daniel was a little boy smiling and cooing at the mirror image. "Look, Bumble Bee, that's you." Both images were smiling back at him. Daniel tried to remember who the man was, but he couldn't. He was trying to figure out if this was a dream. As he reached to touch the young man's face, his hand hit something metallic, and Daniel's eyes popped open. He carefully wiped his eyes with his T-shirt, trying to avoid any mud.

Daniel's vision grew clearer, and he found he was in a large cavern. A short, troll-like creature was stirring something in a large pot over an open fire on the other side of the room. As he watched the contents boil, it reminded him of scenes of old castles in books and movies.

The troll couldn't have been more than three-and-a-half feet tall. Its large, bulgy arms were hairy and longer than normal with boulder-like bulges on its shoulders. Its head had large protrusions all over it with sparse locks of dark hair. Its nose resembled a pig's, and the creature had stubbly hair all over its back. Its clothing looked like the tattered remains of a dress, mostly dirty and muddy. Its legs were bent in the opposite direction of normal human legs, and Daniel didn't see how this thing could lean over the pot like it did. It continued to stir the contents of the pot and didn't seem to notice Daniel.

Daniel began looking around the room, searching for a way to escape. The room was quite large. In the center was a table that looked like it had been outside in the rain too long. Pots and pans hung along the walls. Daniel strained to look inside them. They looked filthy. Metal spoons hung along the walls with the pots and pans. They also looked filthy. Daniel wondered if they had ever been cleaned. In the corner was a pile of bones he hoped were not human. The room smelled rotten. On the wall next to the fireplace hung a dirty mirror. Every so often, the troll leaned over and looked in the mirror, touching its face and nearly nonexistent hair. As Daniel continued to check out the room, he heard the troll with a sweet, sing-song voice say, "It's about time you woke up." The voice sounded familiar, but he couldn't place it.

Daniel tried to stand up and then realized the metal cage

was too small for him to stand up in. It reminded him of birdcages he had seen in medieval movies. This one hung from the ceiling only a foot or so off the floor. Daniel scooted back against the wall of the cage, unable to go any farther. Through the bars, he could touch the nearby wall with its moss and other small plant life growing from it. The glowing ore was not in the wall here.

The troll came close and pulled a narrow chain from around its neck. The chain held two keys. With one of the keys, the troll unlocked the cage door and opened it. Then it backed up to allow Daniel to exit the cage.

When Daniel came out and stood up, he noticed he was almost two feet taller than the troll. He considered the bulk of the troll and imagined he could outrun it easily. Daniel remembered joking with his mom about being able to outrun her. He smiled at the thought of his realized advantage.

The troll took a bony finger and poked it at Daniel, uttering, "You need more meat on your bones. Come. Sit. Have something." The troll pointed at the table, picked up a nasty bowl, and poured some of the stew into it. Handing it to Daniel and motioning to the table, the troll said, "Sit. Sit." When Daniel failed to move, it motioned at the table one more time. Daniel always did as he was told, and as much as he hated using the filthy utensils, he was hungry, so he took a sip of the soup. Although it didn't taste very good, Daniel was too hungry to care. He ate it all.

When the bowl was empty, the troll asked Daniel if he wanted more. Daniel said, "No, thank you." The troll picked up the bowl, refilled it anyway, and then replaced the bowl in front of him. Daniel ate the contents of this bowl as well.

The troll picked up the bowl and spoon, and laughed, "There's more where that came from."

Daniel watched the troll hang the spoon and bowl back up on the wall without washing them. Then the troll moved to the mirror as if peering into it again. The bulges on top of the troll's shoulders lifted up and seemed to whisper in the troll's ears. They pointed at the reflection and said how ugly it was. They also made other vile comments about the appearance of the reflection. Daniel continued to watch the exchange for a moment, and then he got up to investigate the pot. An eyeball rose to the surface and seemed to turn and look at him. It was all he could do to keep from throwing up.

Daniel turned his head, continuing to look around. There were two openings on opposite ends of the room. Both had the soft, glowing minerals, but Daniel had no idea which opening was the way out. Once more he felt lost and alone.

The troll poked its spoon toward Daniel. "Don't you be thinking about running off. You belong to me." The troll pointed the spoon at the cage on the other side of the room. "That's where you'll be sleeping tonight until I'm ready."

Daniel thought, *Ready for what?*

The troll went over to the cage and unlocked it. Then it instructed Daniel to get inside. If Daniel could think of a way to get away and a place to run to, he could surely outrun this short troll. But once again, he did what he was told. He knew that was what he always did. He got inside the cage, and the

The Cave

troll locked the door. Daniel's stomach began to turn as he thought about what was in the stew. *This is not what I wanted! This is not my life! This is not right!*

Daniel avoided watching the troll stirring the pot. Instead, he began to look around to see if there was a way to escape before he became part of the pot as well. The walls were slimy and dark with a bit of plants growing on them that resembled tiny mushrooms. He could taste them and get sick, or maybe they would make him feel better. He didn't feel like there was much to lose, so he reached up and plopped a mushroom into his mouth. It tasted good. He waited to see if his stomach would start churning. Ten minutes passed and then 20—it felt like an entire hour. He felt better, and his stomach did not hurt. At least he had something to eat besides that nasty stew, although he knew that the more he ate, the quicker he would get himself into the stew. He had to do something to get away. He watched the troll stir the coals, encouraging the flames until they responded. The troll used the same poker to stir the stew. The troll said, "Adds flavor." Daniel didn't know why the troll was talking to him. He was not aware of any practice of talking to your food. The troll pointed to the mushrooms on the wall and the other plants growing there. It even pointed to a slug. "If you're hungry enough, you can eat them. You don't get sick; nobody gets sick here."

Daniel was unsure if he wanted to trust anything the troll told him. He sat and watched the troll. He didn't know how long. There was no sun, no clocks, no sense of time. He just sat and watched as the troll went about its business. Occasionally, the troll stopped and pointed at Daniel, encouraging him to eat a little more. Daniel was not willing to do so. Finally, the boredom was too much, and Daniel drifted off to sleep.

"Bumble Bee, where are you? I can't find you. Bumble Bee, help me find you!" Daniel opened his eyes. He was still in the cage hanging in this dirty, dank, muddy place. Would he ever be able to go home?

Daniel heard the cage unlock and turned to brace himself. When the cage was almost open, he forced his legs against the door, knocking the troll backward. He quickly climbed out of the cage and pushed the troll down. The troll got up clumsily and came after Daniel, waving its spoon in its hand. "It's not time. I'm not ready. Get back." Daniel didn't wait. He pushed the troll one more time toward the fireplace. The soup spilled, and the troll began to scream. Daniel turned to see the troll's clothes on fire as it continued to scream and run back and forth in front of the fire. Daniel ran toward an opening in the far wall and turned the corner. He took a moment to lean against the wall and listen. He could hear the troll's screams, but they were not getting louder. He was safe at last.

As Daniel stood there, the minerals began to change from a soft white to a bright blue. This new color appeared to move along the wall, brighten, and then dim. It seemed to move down the tunnel and back into the cave. "What?" whispered Daniel. "Should I go back to the troll?" The light continued to point the way back to the cave room. "I hope this isn't from the mushrooms," Daniel added.

Slowly Daniel began to trace his steps. When he reached

the room, he looked inside to find the troll sitting next to the fire and crying. "I was just doing what I thought was right," it wailed.

Across the room, Daniel saw the blue light appear in the opposite tunnel opening. As Daniel advanced, he kept watching the troll. As he was walking past the troll, he noticed it was chained to a metal ring embedded in the floor next to the fire. He also noticed that the troll was wearing a pair of dirty, pink, fuzzy house shoes. They were muddy and matted, but the color was unmistakable. Daniel thought about the second key on the troll's chain and took the chain from the troll's neck. The troll hung its head. "You can take it. It belongs to you anyway."

Knowing the troll could follow him if he let him go, Daniel still handed the troll the key. "I think this was provided for you. It may be the answer you are looking for. Try it on your chains. Find the way out of your prison." Daniel smiled at the troll as it looked up with wonder.

Then Daniel leaned over to whisper in the troll's ear. "You are not as vile as they claim you are. Stop listening to them."

The troll looked up at Daniel, smiled, and accepted the key from his hand.

Daniel turned, entered the second dirt corridor, and followed the blue light. The corridors were growing larger, and the temperature wasn't nearly as hot. He finally entered another large room. In the room were three large doors. He was going home. But which door should he choose? He stood before the trio of doors, reciting the old nursery rhyme out loud—"eeny, meeny, miny, moe." Then he reached for a door and opened it. Stepping through, he saw a hypnotic star field. Suddenly, he was on the other side. Someone had slammed into him, knocking him down.

"What now?" he exclaimed.

CHAPTER 7

Jessica's Door

Eric, the boy from school who was after Jessica, had managed to worm his way into the good graces of her parents, Mr. and Mrs. Truman, who lived in the house next door. At first, it had been difficult, but after Mrs. Truman's illness, it had been easy for Eric to convince Mr. Truman of his sincere friendship and support of their daughter, Jessica.

Today, Jessica's father had taken his wife to another medical appointment, leaving Jessica alone. Eric decided to stop by, courtesy of quite a bit of liquid courage. Jessica snuck out of the house, hoping Eric didn't notice.

As she ran down the street, she heard Eric taunting her. "You can run, but you can't hide. I will find you." His words slurred through the booze and drugs. She could picture the crooked, droopy smile on Eric's face. She shuddered, imagining his face marred by the chemicals racing through his veins.

Jessica continued to run along the sidewalk, wiping her eyes. Bam! She ran right into her neighbor, Mrs. Bechtel, nearly toppling them both to the ground. "Dear me, child. Where are you going in such a hurry?" Mrs. Bechtel didn't appear to notice the tears on Jessica's face. She glanced at the Truman house, but nothing seemed out of the ordinary. Neither of them noticed the large, dark shadow overhead coming down the street toward them.

Jessica smiled sheepishly and stammered, "Oh, nowhere. I just thought I might try jogging a little and was really in the zone. I guess my music was a little loud."

Mrs. Bechtel looked but didn't see any earbuds or a cord. She smiled and glanced up again at Jessica's house. "Jessica, would you like to come in for a soda?"

"No, ma'am," replied Jessica. She had enough experience with people who seemed nice in public and not so nice in private. Besides, she noticed Mrs. Bechtel looking toward her home and wasn't sure what that meant.

"Well," said Mrs. Bechtel, resting her hand on Jessica's shoulder and leaning down to look deep into Jessica's eyes. "Be safe, and remember, your safety lies in those who lead you. Be careful who you follow, and know there are some you can have faith in." Mrs. Bechtel tilted her head and smiled a big smile that seemed to wrap Jessica in a warm blanket. Then Mrs. Bechtel turned and walked up the steps of her porch and into her house.

Jessica's eyes followed Mrs. Bechtel's retreat into the house, wondering what the woman meant. For a moment, she considered following Mrs. Bechtel but decided that would be rude.

Jessica's Door

Jessica scanned the yard and noticed that Mrs. Bechtel had left her backyard gate open. It would be the neighborly thing to close it for her. As Jessica reached the gate, she thought she heard Eric calling her name rather faintly. Without thinking, she silently moved to the inside of the gate and into Mrs. Bechtel's backyard, gently closing the gate behind her. Looking around, she saw a small garden shed and decided to hide inside it. Once inside, she closed the door as firmly as she could and looked for a lock on the door. She found none. Hoping Eric wouldn't look there, she moved as far into the back of the little shed as she could.

"I saw you," Eric chimed from the gate into Mrs. Bechtel's backyard. "You can't hide. Come out, come out wherever you are!" The shed door began to rattle. Jessica heard a muffled voice and Eric responding, "You just go back inside, Mizz Bechamel. Jessica is my 'sponsibility. You stay out of it." There was more of the other muffled voice. "You go ahead and call the cops," Eric proclaimed. "I can get to you before they can." A door slammed.

Jessica sat down and scooted farther into the back of the dark shed. She cried quietly, "Help me!" She didn't realize she was sitting on a wooden, slatted trap door until it opened, dropping her into a dark, damp crawl space only large enough for her to lie flat on her back. As she looked up through the slats, the trap closed without making a sound, locking her beneath the shed.

The latch on the door to the shed cracked and broke away. The door flew open, and Eric pushed in. His eyes searched the small shed as he stood in the doorway. Inside, he began moving things around and tapped his foot on the floor. "I'm gonna find you," he sang softly.

Jessica looked up through the floorboards. Slits of light shone through from the late afternoon sunshine. It was reflecting off the dust floating down through the slats. Jessica held her breath, and everything grew quiet. Footsteps crossed back across the floor above her and stopped at the door. Eric scanned the shed one more time before going back out the shed door. Finally, he closed the door, leaving Jessica in the dark.

Jessica pushed up on the trap door, but nothing happened. She grabbed a few of the boards and shook them with the same result. Reexamining the boards revealed no door at all. She lowered her arms back to the floor of the small crawl space and looked at the floorboards above her. Gradually, letters begin to glow blue on the boards.

•••

Do not sing of your victory, dear enemy. When my foot slips, it will regain its foothold. When I find myself in darkness, my King will be a light to me.

•••

Jessica called out, "Yeah, don't sing, Eric!" She quickly covered her mouth, hoping Eric hadn't heard her. Then the glowing words faded, leaving her in the dark again. "Now what?" she whispered to herself.

A soft, blue light began to form above Jessica's head.

Twisting to look toward its source, she saw what appeared to be a narrow tunnel. Not knowing what else to do, she carefully crawled toward the light to see what was causing it. She scooted what seemed like a long way through mud, then dry ground, and more muck. The tunnel seemed to grow in size until she reached an opening to a large, cavernous room. The sides of the room sloped down toward the center. The ceiling high above was covered with stalactites, but the opposing stalagmites beneath them appeared to have been cut at a height that made them ideal for sitting. The center of the cavern was empty and gave the appearance of a meeting place. When Jessica looked again, she saw a bright, blue, glowing orb hovering in the center of the room. She slowly moved toward the orb. Her foot slipped a few times on the slick rock beneath her along the edges of the chamber, but she caught herself and found sure footing as she moved toward the center and the glowing, blue orb.

As Jessica approached the orb, it began to grow into the image of a person. It was dressed in armor, reminding her of a knight from King Arthur's Roundtable. "Are you real?" she asked. "What are you?"

Approaching the glowing image, she saw a crown atop the headgear. The image didn't answer her but turned and began walking down another large tunnel. Darkness began to engulf Jessica as the knightly King walked away. She remembered these glowing words: *When in darkness, the King will be a light.* Then there was Mrs. Bechtel telling her something about being careful who she placed her faith in. She remembered that her mother had often talked about a King who once saved her. Was this that King?

    Jessica paused only a moment before moving quickly to catch up and follow the King. His blue glow led her through a maze of tunnels to another large room. The walls of the room had veins of blue light reflecting in them, but the Knight was nowhere to be seen. Along the walls of the room were three solid, wooden doors, each without adornment. "Now what?" Jessica asked. She thought she heard a soft, still voice saying, "One leads home. The other two lead to adventures with the King. Which one do you choose?" The blue crystals in the wall above the third door began to glow a little brighter. "I hope this one leads to adventure," she whispered to herself. Then she opened the door and stepped through it. The world around her became a swirl of stars and rainbow colors as she fell.

CHAPTER 8

A Strange World

Jessica exited the tunnel of light and entered a strange jungle. At once she was knocked down. As she spat fresh leaves out of her mouth, she turned to see Daniel sitting on the ground next to her.

"What are you doing here?" Daniel asked her.

"I could ask you the same thing." Jessica appeared unsettled. "I was trying to find my way home, but apparently these doors have a mind of their own." Jessica rubbed her shoulder. Daniel figured that was where she had collided with him.

Both looked around. All they could see were large leaves on stalks growing out of the ground. It reminded Daniel of a plant growing in front of Gigi's house. But there were no doors. "Either these plants are extra large or we are very small," Daniel said. "This feels like *Honey, I Shrunk the Kids*." Daniel looked up and laughed nervously.

Jessica looked around. "If it is, we're in big trouble. Better watch out for Lego pieces and giant bugs." They smiled at the thought of the movie and hopefully at the absurdity of their situation.

The leaves began to rustle and part, revealing Alex Rodriguez running toward them. He was out of breath, and his face and arms below his T-shirt sleeves were covered in large welts. "How did you get here?" Jessica asked. "Alex, what happened to your face and arms?"

Alex looked around in the leaves and answered, "I thought I was dreaming when I ran into a bunch of something that someone called Stingers. At least that's what the weird talking beetle called them. Then a bunch of huge blackbirds came swooping in and began eating them. I ran because I didn't want the birds to think I was a Stinger, a beetle, or whatever they were. How did you two get here?"

Jessica replied, "I went through a door, and when I came through it, Daniel mowed me down." Jessica crossed her arms and waited for Daniel to answer the charges.

"Same thing for me," Daniel smiled sheepishly, "only I sort of fell through."

A soft purr erupted through the leaves. The light above had dimmed but was just bright enough so they could see a sleek, black cat standing on two back legs. It pushed through the leaves and stepped into the clearing and the light of the full moon. "Welcome to m-m-my world," she softly purred. "We get unusual visitors like you every s-s-so often. Did you also come through a portal? I can help you survive here if you like. There are many of us-s-s. We all look a little different, but don't be afraid. My name is Catrina." The cat-like creature smiled at

A Strange World

them as she licked the back of her furry paw and rubbed the fur on the side of her face with it. Daniel, Jessica, and Alex looked at each other with wide eyes.

"Thank you," Jessica replied. "We are new here. Where exactly is 'here'?"

Catrina just giggled. "Follow me. We have a place where you can meet the others."

Daniel, Alex, and Jessica asked together, "Others?"

Unsure of their next move, they followed Catrina as she turned and began spreading a pathway through the plants, her tail swishing from side to side as she walked deeper into their jungle-like surroundings.

Jessica leaned over to Daniel. "If she's a cat and is our size, maybe we are small." Daniel wasn't sure if Jessica was trying to be funny or not. He thought about it for a moment and decided that either way, it wasn't funny.

As they moved through the plants, Daniel noticed a faint, orange glow ahead of them. As they grew closer, the glow turned into a campfire where several other teenagers were sitting on upended logs around it. Among the teenagers was the easily recognizable form of Justin and his friends. They all had large welts on their faces. "What is this? Why have you brought us here?" Daniel angrily asked Catrina. The others around didn't seem to notice Daniel's concern. Justin made no move toward Daniel, so Daniel decided he would ignore Justin as well.

Daniel continued looking around the circle of kids. He recognized many of them, but some he did not. Daniel wondered, *How did they get here? How did any of them get here? Why are any of them here?* Daniel waved at some of the other kids from his school, but they seemed to barely notice him. Many kept looking at the foliage around them. "This place has that effect on people," Catrina purred, standing next to Daniel.

Daniel had about all he could take. *I don't want to be here*, he thought. *Why can't we all just go home?'* Daniel looked around at the group of kids as he continued his thoughts. *No, I'm not going to let this place get to me. There has to be a way* out.

Suddenly, without warning, a strand of blue light whipped through the underbrush and wrapped itself around one of the girls who was sitting on a log in the circle. It pulled her into the dense plants, and she was gone. No one was sure how to react. Most of the kids were in shock as they looked around at each other. Once again, the blue cord of bright light reached from the foliage and grabbed another kid. They vanished into the leaves. The light strand grabbed two more kids, and they were gone.

Catrina was standing in the center of the circle close to the campfire with one paw near her face and the other pointing. She was shivering. "This is your fault!" she screamed. Daniel turned to see who she was pointing at. There was no one there. They must have also been taken.

A young, petite Asian girl who Daniel had not noticed before stood up and spoke matter-of-factly. "Many are called, but few are chosen," she said. The kids all turned and stared at her.

Then Catrina began to hiss and moved to attack the Asian

girl. Suddenly, a large lion appeared from the jungle behind the Asian girl and pounced on Catrina. She screamed, "Help me!" Only the Asian girl moved toward her.

The Asian girl screamed back at Catrina, "No, it's your fault they are here. It's your fault they have been taken. You will pay for this!"

The lion pinned down Catrina and then began making a deep, purr-like roar. Daniel felt a tingling in his brain, and the images around him began to shift. When he looked back at the pair on the ground in front of him, he saw that Catrina's face was distorted, almost melting into something hideous. Her fur appeared charred.

Daniel turned to look at the others standing around him. They were staring at Catrina and the lion. The Asian girl stood next to the lion. Justin's friend Alonzo spoke up. "I don't want to be here. I don't want this." With that, the long, thin strand of blue light whipped around Alonzo and pulled him into the forest.

Justin looked up at Daniel. "What's happening here?" He pointed at the Asian girl. "What does she mean about being called and chosen?" Daniel looked at Justin. The welts on his face were almost gone. Justin continued, "I demand that somebody tell me what is happening!" He was visibly shaking at this point.

The Asian girl spoke first. "My name is Kia. This is my host," pointing at the lion. "His name is Dominion." Then Dominion released Catrina and stepped back to stand next to Kia. Catrina slowly got up on all fours, checking to see if anyone was watching. When no one moved toward her, she ran into the forest. No one followed her.

Kia rested her hand on Dominion's back and scratched him affectionately. Dominion spoke in a low, gruff voice. "I am not your pet, little one." Kia laughed and released her hand from his back. Then Dominion shook his head, which made his mane swirl around him.

"Why did he melt and burn Catrina?" Daniel asked.

Kia responded, "He didn't do anything to Catrina. The Darkness has the ability to distort what you see. Dominion removed her influence on your mind."

Jessica quipped, "How do we know you two aren't influencing our minds?"

"Well," Kia smirked, "I guess you'll have to decide who you want to trust, won't you?" Jessica took a step backward. The others stared at them. No one else spoke. Kia shrugged her shoulders. "This world is different. You need to get used to things here. They are not as they seem."

Daniel perked up, remembering what Gigi had told him just days earlier—or was it only a day? It had seemed so long since he first fell through the portal in Gigi's closet. Gigi would be excited to know her portal worked. But what had brought him here, and how was he going to get home?

Kia pointed to the forest around them. "This is the King's territory, at least the untamed part." Kia paused and drew a breath. "We have all found our way here differently, but we *are* here. The creatures here are sometimes familiar and sometimes very strange. Some will protect you, and many want only to hurt you." Kia paused and took a long breath. "Let me explain."

Kia turned to all of them and said, "Long ago, before humans existed, there were Love, the King, and the Light. Love designed the creatures; the King and the Light created them. They were all servants of the King. One of the creatures they created was above all the others. He was stronger, larger, and more beautiful. But this servant believed he was more.

"Then he learned about the design of a final creature. It was to be a child of Love—weak, small, and sometimes ugly. He became enraged. He managed to turn many of the creatures he had authority over against Love, the King, and Light. It was, and is, his desire to annihilate this inferior creature and overthrow Love. But Love knew about his plans and threw them all out of the palace. Now they roam this dimension and try to terrorize the final creature.

"It is up to you to decide which creatures are trying to help you and which are not, especially because those who are not will most likely want to harm you or kill you." Kia paused to let her words sink in. "Love calls us to help him defeat the Evil One, but we must decide to cooperate with Love. Those called who are willing to fight the Evil One are chosen to complete the task."

Daniel spoke first. "So how were we called, and how do we *not* get chosen? Personally, I would like to go home and get back to my normal life."

Kia shook her head and began to walk around the inside

of the circle of kids. "But that's just it. No life is normal if the Evil One is seeking you. You are in grave danger, as is your whole family and everyone you care about. Evil is trying to change things and gain control of the final creature. We can't let that happen. Please consider helping us, mostly because it will reflect in your world as well. If Evil succeeds, all will change for the worst in both dimensions. As bad as things are, if we don't succeed, it will only continue to get worse—much worse."

Kia walked in the circle around the campfire. "We constantly look at the bad things that happen and say, 'Oh well, it's part of the King's grand plan.' But it isn't his plan for bad things to happen to us. We are here to thrive. We are told in the Book to be fruitful and multiply. That is not a plan for evil, pain, and destruction. That plan comes from the mind of man and his poor choices. Love, not Evil, is the source of all good things. Love is Jireh, the source of the Light. He is pure love and supplies all we need, but the Darkness wishes to steal what we should have, destroy what is ours, and kill anything it can. That is the source of Evil in your worlds, the source of the Darkness in each of us. Love's plans for us are good. The Darkness, the Evil, changes those plans because the Darkness hates the Light. He hates Love, and he hates you. Yet the King's love works to bring everything to our good if we are willing to love him back. He can make something evil into something good if we are willing to listen to his instruction. He loves for us to work with him. He expects it." Kia sat back and stared at the flames of the fire.

Jessica sat watching Kia. "How do I know if I am hearing from the King?"

Kia pulled a cylindrical object from her pocket and handed it to Jessica. "Here. Point it up, and press the button on the side."

Jessica took the object. While holding it up, she pressed the button Kia had pointed to. An image appeared in front of her with soft, blue letters.

Most importantly, little one, keep your mind on truth: those things that are noble, right, pure, if it is lovely or admirable—anything of excellence or worthy of praise— think about these things.

Kia continued. "When we focus on this, it is easier to hear his promptings and distinguish him from the Darkness, which is always trying to interfere and draw us away from Light. It's a good place to start to get your heart and mind in a place to hear."

Daniel's brow furrowed. "How do you know all this?"

Kia replied, "I had a nurse, I mean nanny, who taught me about this place. She was a daughter of the King, and from her teachings, I became a daughter of the King too. When my parents found out, they fired her, but I remember what she taught me. About a year ago, the King himself came and brought me through the first door. I have learned even more since then. I come often to help him with rescue missions. He is so wonderful. I'm sure you will get to meet him too." Kia's smile stretched across her face.

Daniel sat quietly trying to understand what Kia had told him. He wasn't sure what he believed about Kia's journey, but this world was testing many of his own beliefs.

Jessica spoke next. "I know what she is talking about. I have seen this myself but was not willing to admit it. It makes sense that it is happening everywhere, not just here. We've been given an opportunity to make this world better, including our own in the process." With that, Jessica stood next to Kia. "I'm in. Who's with me?"

Kia smiled and ruffled Dominion's mane, which he shook, dislodging her hand. Timothy Garza, one of Justin's goons at school, scanned the group. "Now what? Where do we go from here? I understand about fighting an enemy, but this fight isn't a fair one. We have no cover and no weapons."

Kia jumped up and said, "Leave that to me and Dominion. First, we must make our way to the other side of the valley. There is a waterfall and another portal just behind it. From there we will see where the King leads us. Come on." Kia waved her arm to indicate that they should follow her. No one moved.

"Why can't we wait until morning?" asked a tall, skinny girl. Daniel hadn't noticed her before, but he remembered her from school. She had been one of Samantha Harris' friends. He remembered that her name was Karen something.

Kia stopped and turned to face the girl. "The planet is

covered in an ice shield, but the core is very warm, which gives moisture and the proper temperature for vegetation and life to grow. The sun and moon rotate with the planet, so very little light reaches here. There is no morning. And the cliff walls also block the sun. This valley is hidden from the sky. We must travel now before the Stingers come back and more of us look like Timothy, Justin, and Alex. Now who's ready to go?"

"That's not physically possible," interjected Justin.

Kia responded to everyone. "This is not the dimension you came from. Your sciences don't always apply here. You must get used to the possibility of something different." She walked to Justin and rested her hand on his shoulder. "You are brave and courageous. Don't let your hurts shadow the King's truths." She then moved to the edge of the clearing and faced the others. Looking at Karen, she said, "Now, are we ready?"

Karen nodded, and everyone moved closer to Kia. Soon, all were in line to begin the journey with Karen and Daniel bringing up the rear.

As the others began the journey to the waterfall, Jessica thought she heard someone call her name. When she turned around, the Blue Knight was standing behind her. Excitedly, she ran to hug him. "I'm so glad I got to see you again!" Jessica exclaimed.

"You said you wanted the adventure and to help others like your mother did," he said softly.

"I did say that! You heard me?" Jessica replied quietly.

"Yes, of course I did. And if you meant it, I have a quest for you that only you can carry out, but only if you want to." The Knight paused for Jessica's response.

Jessica looked into the eyes of the knightly King and smiled. "I do want to. What is it?"

"You will see," answered the King. "Now take these items. You will need them on this quest." The King smiled back at Jessica who held out her hand and took the small objects from the knightly King.

Jessica turned to look at the others heading through the brush. "What about the others?" she asked. But when she looked back at the King, he was gone. In her hand were earbuds, a pin, and a cord. She looked again for the King, but he was truly gone. She placed the objects in her pocket and ran to follow the others.

CHAPTER 9
Nabuta

They were close to the far edge of the valley. Daniel could hear the roar of the waterfall and smell the humidity in the air. The next portal was near. It was then that the insect-like Stingers attacked. They were about five inches long with broad wings that moved very fast like a dragonfly's. Their body had tiny scales, and at the head was what resembled a human face. At the other end were rings with a long stinger. They were attacking and stinging the kids wherever there was unprotected skin.

The teenagers were running around trying to swat the Stingers. Alex broke a large leaf off one of the plants growing along the path and was using it to swat at the Stinger that was attacking him. Daniel wasn't sure if Alex's swatting tactic was working. Dominion seemed to be jumping, biting, or maybe eating the Stingers.

Over the screams of the others, Daniel could barely hear Kia's instructions. "Run for the falls. They are not far.

Just don't stop on the way, and definitely do not enter any structures or buildings. Come on! Hurry! We can make it if we stay together!"

Suddenly, a cat-like creature stood in front of Daniel. "No, Catrina, I won't listen to you. I know you are here to bring harm. I saw you burn before." Daniel stiffened his stance before the creature. Karen had stopped next to him.

"I don't know what you are talking about," the creature snapped at Daniel. "I have never been through the fire," she smirked. "You must be referring to my sister, Catrina. Oh, yes! She's the evil one." She softened her tone. "My name is Purrsyfoni. I'm not like her. You can trust me. Come. I know how to get away from the stingers. Come quickly!" Purrsyfoni motioned with urgency.

Then Karen responded. "I'm coming. Anything to get out of this mess."

Daniel shrugged and followed Karen. Along their retreat, several other students followed to the sanctuary that Purrsyfoni promised. Timothy Garza was one of them. "Hey, should we tell the others we've found a safe place?" he asked.

Daniel hesitated and was hit by a Stinger. "No!" he screamed. "I'm not getting any more bites. I'm going. Do what you want to," he shouted as he turned to follow the small group of kids.

It was not long before Purrsyfoni parted the leaves, revealing a large pyramid. She led them inside. Once all had entered the structure, the door closed behind them and disappeared, leaving a solid wall. Then Purrsyfoni led them to a large, open chamber. Twenty-one narrow, stone chairs with tall backs formed a circle in the middle of the room. Several other kids were already there. They sat straight, unmoving. Only four chairs remained empty. As Daniel, Karen, and Timothy looked around, they recognized a few kids from their town. The others were from somewhere else.

"What is this place?" Daniel asked Purrsyfoni.

"The council of the great one," she replied. "He is building a new council from the youth of your town and surrounding cities. Not everyone is called like you and your friends. You are special. That's why he chose you."

"Why are we chosen?" questioned Timothy.

"It's your willingness to follow, of course, and your ability to convince others," purred Purrsyfoni. "Hurry. Sit. You are the last to arrive. Nabuta will be here soon."

At that moment, a large creature entered the chamber. He stood almost 10 feet tall and had a thin frame. He was wrapped in a black, flowing cloak that bellowed behind him as he walked. His sleeves stretched to his wrists with three spiny, narrow fingers sticking out from their ends. His head was dark and oval with a bulbous cranium. His wrinkled face was small and narrow with glassy, black eyes. There were holes for breathing along with a thin mouth near the bottom. Above his face were horns that twisted as they reached outward and upward from beneath his hood. He walked on two hairy legs with hooves at the end. Daniel thought about the Minotaur on his computer game at home.

The creature's crooked frame crossed the room, casting odd

shadows as he moved. Clearing his throat, he spoke in a low, gravelly voice. "I am Nabuta. I am so glad you are here. Soon we will have our council of 21 children from your area. These 21 must not have been influenced by false words of this cosmic battle beyond your world. It's a battle of the multi-verse! You are here to wage war in your own world, to protect us—and you, of course."

"One of the kids raised his hand and asked, "How will we do this? We're only kids."

"I will teach you," Nabuta continued. "You will learn to use the power of this world to change your own, to control it." Nabuta raised his hand into the air as if to emphasize his power.

One of the kids Daniel did not know stood to accept Nabuta's offer. He said, "I want to protect my town. What do we have to do?"

"Excellent!" Nabuta responded. "Now who else will join me?"

Daniel turned to look at Timothy who was looking back at him and slowly shaking his head. Timothy was right. They should have listened to Kia and headed for the waterfall. She had warned them that the Stingers would attack and instructed them not to enter any structures. She had been right. She and Dominion were the ones they should have trusted. Now what? How were they going to get out of this? What would Nabuta say or, worse, do if they refused his offer?

Timothy stood up. Daniel tried to get him to sit back down, but Timothy spoke instead. "I don't choose to follow you. I don't believe you are trying to protect us or our cities. I ask that you release those who choose not to join you."

Nabuta laughed. "What makes you think you have a choice in the matter? You belong to me and will do as I say. If you do not, you will feel the power of my wrath." Nabuta started creating a circling motion with his right hand and speaking in guttural sounds. Timothy grabbed his stomach and doubled over in pain. Many of the kids sat shaking, and then one by one, they stood and pledged their allegiance to Nabuta. Daniel stayed seated, unsure of what to do. He then stood up and moved to Timothy's side.

"I wish Dominion were here. He'd melt that Nabuta like a paper doll." Daniel laughed softly as he held Timothy's shoulders. Timothy smiled but didn't stop rocking from the pain.

Daniel turned to look at the others. Nabuta continued. "I will teach you how to control your enemies and how to inflict pain and bring them to their knees. No one will be able to stop you. You will have great power. I will be your king. I will teach you everything you need to know. Our coven of 21 will be all-powerful and will control the evil in your town. You will be my army of destruction. You will not regret following me." A smile formed on Nabuta's grotesque face.

Daniel turned back to Timothy who spoke over his pain. "I follow the true King. You are only a follower of lies."

Daniel whispered, "I will follow the King of all as well. May he forgive me for turning away from his instructions and bringing Timothy here with me." Daniel and Timothy could hear the sound of sparklers near them. As they looked around, an electrifying dot appeared next to them. It grew larger and larger, becoming a circle. Waves like water seemed to fill the circle. Daniel thought it looked like a portal he had once seen in a movie. Nabuta and the others stepped back from it in horror. When it had grown large enough, Dominion sprang through it, and the portal snapped closed. Dominion stood between the two boys and the others. His roar was deafening. As he roared, he grew twice the size of Nabuta and moved to the center of the chamber. Nabuta, Purrsyfoni, and the others in the room who had pledged allegiance to Nabuta clung to the opposite wall.

Dominion turned to Daniel and Timothy. "Climb up." Daniel and Timothy were shaken but complied as quickly as they were able. Dominion turned to face the others pressed against the far wall. "Does anyone else refuse the mastery of Nabuta? If so, come with me now. This may be your last chance." Dominion waited as Karen stepped forward. Dominion growled, "Do not try to deceive. There has been evil in your heart since you came to this place."

Karen stepped forward, still shaking. "I have been forced to do what I have done. I now renounce the Evil One and wish to follow the King." She held her head high before Dominion.

"Very well," he replied. "You will have many opportunities to reinforce your decision." Turning to Nabuta, Dominion stated, "Do not try to follow. You are but a shadow, a mirage, a paper float to symbolize something strong. You are not. One day I will be allowed to crush you. One day." Nabuta shook as though he was trying to control his anger—or was it fear? Daniel couldn't tell.

Karen, along with Daniel and Timothy, climbed up on Dominion and grabbed his furry mane. Daniel helped Timothy hold on to Dominion's furry main and back. Suddenly, Dominion unfolded large, white wings that were covered with what seemed like a million eyes. Wrapping the wings around himself and his riders, he stood on his hind legs and stretched to the ceiling. His body began to transform into a rocket ship as a new portal appeared above them. When it was large enough, Dominion shot through it.

Nabuta stepped to the center of the chamber and looked at the diminishing hole. "Why do I always have to rebuild my council?" Turning to face the others, Nabuta added, "Please, be seated. We will begin our lessons soon. Purrsyfoni, go find new replacements." Nabuta sneered at her. "This time make sure they are not familiar with the King and his ways." Purrsyfoni cowered and slipped out the door that had reappeared.

Once outside, Dominion spread his wings and glided down to the waterfall where the others waited. After the three disembarked, Daniel turned to thank a more normal-sized Dominion, assuming this was his normal size. Dominion looked at Daniel, nodded, and smiled. Daniel spoke first. "Thank you, Dominion. I don't know how you knew, but thank you."

"It's a good thing you called for Dominion," Kia said. "Otherwise, there's no telling what would have happened." Kia looked at Daniel and smiled.

"How did he hear us?" Daniel asked.

"The King hears and knows all. The King sent Dominion. You really need to believe in the King. He believes in you. That's why you are here." Again, Kia smiled at Daniel who wasn't sure he understood but, as always, went along.

Daniel turned to look for Timothy. He was lying on the stone ground behind the waterfall, facing the water. A blue blanket of light was stretched over him. It appeared to be wrapping itself around him, under him, and even through him. After a moment, Timothy rolled over on his back and sat up. Daniel asked Timothy, "What was that?"

Timothy answered, "It was the Light, the Healing Light. It's part of the father of this realm, Love."

"So the father of this realm is Love, and he has a blue, healing light? How do you know all this stuff?" Daniel asked.

"My aunt and uncle are followers of the King. I never thought much about it until I came here," Timothy answered. "I thought it was just something they made up or that they were in some kind of cult. This is more real than I ever imagined." Looking at Justin, Timothy added, "We all tend to follow something or believe in something. We just need to make sure we know what it is we are following."

Daniel thought about what Timothy said and had to agree. At least he hoped it meant Timothy would no longer bully him.

Kia began speaking. "Okay, everyone, the portal is about to open. It's time to go."

"Go where?" Daniel asked.

Nabuta

"Where the King leads, we follow," Kia said. "I am sure the journey will lead us home. There is much to learn here, but the goal is ultimately to take back with us what we learn. Focus on the discovery, and the rest will follow." Kia seemed sympathetic to the kids' desire to go home. Behind Kia, an open doorway appeared. The world beyond appeared plush with green grass and colorful tents. Just beyond the tents appeared a table of favorite treats. One by one, the kids stepped through to this world of green grass, colorful tents, and delicious food. Daniel and Jessica were the last to step through the door, leaving Kia and Dominion behind. Then the door closed.

CHAPTER 10

Training Begins

Daniel arrived on a grassy slope, but there were no tents and no table of food. Instead, he stood in a large clearing surrounded by trees. Just above the tree line hung a bright, red sun.

In the distance, Daniel saw a puff of purple smoke rising into the sky. He needed answers, and that seemed his most likely source. Walking forward, he noticed that his steps took very little effort. The air was light, cool, and pleasant. He almost felt himself bounce as he moved along the hillside clearing. Within a matter of minutes, he was at a small hut. The thatched, grass roof was at his eye level. Green moss covered the outside walls. A single arched window had flowers growing from the bottom of it without the benefit of a window box.

Daniel approached the window to look inside. A pink peony straightened its stem toward Daniel and said, "Hi! We're so glad you're here. Why don't you come inside?"

Daniel stared at the flower for a moment and then replied,

Training Begins

"I'm not sure I can fit through the door or would be comfortable inside. It looks awfully small."

The peony replied, "You won't know until you try. Besides, the King always tries to make his guests comfortable. Come on in, please."

"The King?" Daniel was surprised at the mention of the King, but it was enough to encourage him to try to enter the little doorway. Daniel moved to the small, red, arched door and turned the thimble-sized knob in its center. He wondered if the King was a Hobbit. Instead of the door opening, he felt himself sucked into it to the room before him.

The room was too low for Daniel to stand up straight. The tiny house was designed for someone smaller than Daniel. It was decorated with items strewn about and looked like storage for antiques, yet it felt comfortable. He smiled and felt as if he had stepped into *Alice in Wonderland*. Suddenly, he fit in the house much better. Even though the house was still too small for him, he wondered if he had just shrunk to fit the house or if the house had grown larger. This place seemed to defy all the laws of nature, but then he wasn't in Kansas, was he?

"Daniel, you came! I wasn't sure you would." Daniel spun around to find a young, blonde girl about the age of five, dressed in a poofy-sleeved, white, lace dress that ended just above a pair of white satin ballet shoes. Daniel had not heard her enter the room.

"Where did you come from?" Daniel asked.

"I was always here; you just didn't see me," she answered.

"Who are you?" Daniel added.

"Oh, no one really. My name is Gabriella. Please come, and have some tea. He is coming soon. I know he will want to see you. Please, come and sit." Gabriella pointed to a chair near Daniel.

"He? Who is *he*?" Daniel asked, turning around to find a suitable chair. "Do you mean the King?" Daniel sat in an overstuffed chair near him. It faced a warm fireplace, the obvious source of the smoke he had seen. Near the chair was a small, wooden table with decorative edges. Around the table were a few other chairs of various designs. They made a very comfortable space to sit and talk with friends. They reminded him of chairs in Gigi's living room—they were old.

"Oh no, you will probably meet him later. The King decided it was time for you to learn the truth. You have a decision to make, and I am hoping you will make the best one. I've been waiting for this moment for so long." Gabriella seemed to giggle with delight in anticipation.

"Waiting? How long have you been waiting? You can't be more than five," Daniel replied.

Gabriella giggled again. "Oh, Daniel, I've been watching you far longer than that. Don't let my size fool you. I've been with you all your life, waiting for you to learn the truth—and believe." Gabriella smiled and sat in a chair across from Daniel, who wondered who she was leaving the chair next to him for. He didn't have to wait long for the answer to the unspoken question.

Suddenly, another door opened. An older gentleman entered carrying a silver platter laden with Daniel's favorite

Training Begins

pastries and three cups of various warm liquids. One looked like hot chocolate. The man set the tray on the table by the chairs and sat in the chair next to Daniel. He slapped his knees and exclaimed, "Well!"

Everyone sat silently for a moment. Gabriella stared at Daniel, smiling. The old man had a large grin on his face as he gazed at Daniel. Daniel stared back. Then the man spoke. "Oh, I am sorry. These are for you. I had them created especially for you. Please indulge yourself. They are all your favorites." The man continued to smile and extended his hand toward the platter.

Daniel looked at the platter and then back at his host. The items were indeed all his favorite items he was seldom able to eat. He kept feeling as though this was all a little too convenient. He had experienced enough tricks on this adventure, and he was not ready to fall for another one.

His host sat back in his chair and said, "That's okay. I know this adventure has been a bit confusing. It is good to question things, especially now. Perhaps I should explain where you are and what is going on." His host paused and sighed before continuing. "My name is Samuel. I was asked to help you understand the reality of this battle we are in and help you with questions you may have."

"First question." Daniel leaned forward in his chair and looked directly at Samuel. "Why am I here? What does this have to do with me? How can I go home? Who am I that everyone keeps treating me like I'm somebody special?" Daniel took a deep breath and relaxed back in his chair.

Samuel smiled. "That's more than one question, but I will do my best to answer all of them. Let me explain. There is a battle between good and evil, the Light and the Darkness."

Daniel interrupted, "There is always a battle between good and evil. We have that on our planet too. What does the battle in your world have to do with me and my world? Why am I here?"

"Daniel," Samuel spoke softly, "your world is part of this world. We are all interconnected. What happens here also happens there. What happens there reflects what happens here. When you fight there, you are only fighting the enemy's pawns. When one pawn falls, the enemy finds another one to use. The less your world knows about the truth, the easier it is for Darkness to use the people of your world. There are many people who choose not to believe in the battle. They go along with their lives, ignoring the warning signs. But that is what the Darkness wants them to do. When they don't choose the Light, they are swallowed up in the Darkness, and he wins."

Daniel stopped Samuel and asked, "What do you mean, *he* wins?"

"Evil wins when you don't choose sides. It isn't a matter of the Darkness defeating the Light. The Light has already defeated the Darkness. It's a matter of defeating you—your kind. We were created before your world was created. We are here to help you. It's more than just you. Your kind is special. You have more potential than even the Darkness, and he knows it."

Training Begins

"Wait," Daniel interrupted again. "Why do you keep referring to the Darkness as *he*?" Daniel was shaking his head.

Samuel answered. "Because Darkness is not just a concept. He is a creature, and he rules over his domain. Right now, his domain is Earth because it was given to him by a man. The authority of it has been regained and given back to man. Now man must choose to take it back from the Evil One's control."

Daniel sat and thought about Samuel's explanations and then asked, "So all we—mankind—have to do is tell the Darkness to leave, and the game is over?"

Samuel chuckled. "If it were only that easy." Samuel drew in a deep breath. "Remember, I told you that some don't believe in the battle between good and evil and that some feel helpless to do anything about it. Well, there are also some who *want* to side with the Darkness. They believe the Darkness gives them power, and they will do anything to keep that power—and I mean *anything*! Imagine a government like that. Think of Hitler, Nero, and Stalin. There are others. They don't want to follow the Light because it would mean losing power, money, and things they consider their gods."

"What do you want me to do about it?" asked Daniel.

"Learn to fight the Darkness." Samuel leaned in toward Daniel and continued. "Understand what is good and what is not so you can tell the difference between them. Learn the truth, practice the truth, have faith in the truth, walk in the peace of the truth, know the truth, and use the truth as your weapon to defeat the enemy. Remember, you don't really fight against the people of your world. Your war is against the Darkness that drives them and the strategies it pushes."

"Okay, how do I train for this war I can't see?" Daniel smiled back at Samuel and winked at Gabriella.

Samuel and Gabriella smiled back. "So you are choosing to follow the King? Is this your decision?" Samuel asked Daniel.

"You choose this with your own free will?" Gabriella added, nearly jumping out of her chair.

Daniel nodded, continuing to smile.

"Please say it, Daniel. Please." Gabriella begged.

Daniel smiled and added, "I choose with my free will to follow the King all the days of my life and protect his kingdom as best I can." With that, Daniel began to laugh—hard.

Samuel stood up and hit his head on the ceiling. Rubbing his head, he exclaimed, "Then your training must start right away."

Samuel and Daniel left the little hut and stood outside. The red sun shone overhead, but the air was not hot. Samuel walked over to Daniel and handed him a wooden, toy sword. "We're fighting with these?" Daniel asked.

Samuel laughed as Daniel swung the toy weapon through the air in front of him. "Only at first," Samuel said. "I promise you will leave here with much more powerful weapons. You must trust me—and the King."

Samuel stood in a fighting stance and began to speak to Daniel. "It is important to remember that we are not here to coexist with evil but to be separated from it and conquer it." Samuel swung his wooden blade at Daniel who blocked it

Training Begins

easily. Samuel stepped back, held his sword up again to prepare for another attack, and stated, "We live in a battle of espionage and warfare every day. It's bigger than the issues between countries. We are part of a greater kingdom that reaches to the farthest corners of this universe. The battle is not just here; it is out there." Samuel stood up straight and pointed to the sky and then pointed at Daniel. "It is on your planet too. In fact, your world is the center of the battle." Daniel swung at Samuel, and Samuel easily blocked his attack.

Samuel continued his instruction as the two continued to attack each other. "You can say there are two worlds—one good and one evil. The people of both worlds live together. What sets the good apart from the evil is who they pledge allegiance to—either the Light or the Darkness. The world of the good is ruled by a benevolent, loving King, A'Primas. The King calls his people 'my children.' He loves them and tries to help them. They are not always willing to accept his help."

Parrying again, Samuel continued. "The world of evil is ruled by a malevolent, hateful Dragon. He is malicious, killing his subjects just because he can. He takes what he can and destroys everything else by getting his most loyal subjects to do it for him. And while the Dragon exerts influence over all the people, he treats the good especially harsh. They, on the other hand, seem bent on ignoring him. This Dragon King has many laws for the people, mostly the laws that define his worship or direct them to obey his commands or orders. The Dragon refers to his people as 'my servants.'"

"Wait," exclaimed Daniel. "What are we doing? This is like

play-fighting with my dad when I was four." Daniel stood with his arms at his sides, facing Samuel. Suddenly, Samuel ran at Daniel with his sword over his head. As the sword came down, Daniel threw up his arms and blocked the assault with his own weapon.

"Was that more interesting?" asked Samuel.

"Um, yeah," replied Daniel.

"Good. Let's continue," replied Samuel.

Daniel lifted his sword, and Samuel lifted his. As they parried, Samuel continued to instruct Daniel. "You need training to analyze and take control of the situation. Remember, you must be cool under pressure. Know your stuff well enough that you do it in your sleep. Don't think; just do." Whack! Whack! The wooden toys struck each other as the pretend fighting continued. "This is not a skill or talent to be learned or developed," Samuel instructed. "It is born of need and faith. It is the one working through you and for you. What you must practice is letting go. Do not trust what you see or feel. Trust him working through you, and focus on his truths."

"Wait!" Daniel held up his hand in a stop motion. "What do you mean 'through you,' and what do you mean by 'faith'?"

Samuel smiled at Daniel's question. "Your strength, your power, and your authority come from the King, and he is the one who works through you. You are not battling under your power, but under his."

"So it's not really a war you can fight with a sword?" Daniel was perplexed.

"No, it isn't," replied Samuel, breathing heavily.

"So why are we doing this?" asked Daniel who was also out of breath.

"Because you expected it," answered Samuel. At this, Daniel dropped his sword. Samuel stepped back and dropped his sword, adding, "Please, let's sit here in the cool grass and continue our instructions." They both sat in the grass, and Gabriella brought more treats from the house and offered them to Samuel and Daniel. Both ate and talked while Gabriella left for the hut.

"So when will I be able to meet the King, or will I ever get to meet him?" Daniel asked as he licked icing from his lips.

"Sometimes, in order to reach the King, we must go through the lowest of valleys, treacherous mountains, rough terrain, and narrow paths of life," Samuel answered. "Do not be deceived into believing that the supreme ruler of the Universe is ignoring you. That is a lie of the Evil One. Not only is he not ignoring you, but he also has the ability to do whatever you are asking of him. Never forget that. It will sustain you."

Daniel looked up from his cup of cocoa and tried to peer into the woods in front of him. He tried to remember the plaque in Gigi's kitchen. *What did it say about who we are fighting?* Daniel turned and asked Samuel, "So how do we fight this evil?"

"The King will guide you and give you knowledge on how to do that," Samuel said. "Remember this, Daniel." Some people think the evil is not that bad and the good is not that good. They believe there isn't much difference between the two."

"Why would people think that?" questioned Daniel.

"I only know that many are deceived by the Darkness and the promises it makes, even though Darkness has no desire to keep its part of the promise. Sometimes these followers of evil pretend to be good in order to get others to trust them so they can easily deceive them to defeat the plans of A'Primas. That has happened to your friends. They need your help. This time the battle has come to you."

With that, they rose, and a door appeared in the field before them. Samuel pointed at the door for Daniel to enter. "Wait! Gigi talked about armor. When will I get mine?"

Samuel answered Daniel. "Ask the King. It is not hidden from you but is hidden for you. Continue to search. He will show you. May the Light go with you, Daniel. Farewell." Daniel stepped through the door before him.

CHAPTER 11

Jessica's Quest

Jessica looked around, unsure of what had just happened. Stepping through the door was not what she had expected. There were no beautiful trees, no grass, and no pools of sparkling blue water. There was, in fact, no water or vegetation at all. There was only sand as far as she could see.

She squatted on the sand, trying to get her bearings. Where were the others? They had all gone through the same doorway, but no one else was with her on this side. Like the trees, the grass, and the water, the other kids were also gone! When she turned to look for the door, it had disappeared. There was no evidence of the door through which she had just stepped.

Jessica tried to remember her last steps. She recalled the beautiful, brown door with its ornate metalwork and thought about the lush green she was sure she saw on the other side. She had watched each individual step through, but when she stepped through, everything changed. Had it been a trick? Was the beautiful garden fake? If so, what had happened to the others? Maybe she just couldn't see them.

Jessica called out to the group, but no one responded. She was alone. Fear began to creep over her like a cold blanket. Thoughts began to run through her brain. *The King has deserted you. He did this to you. You're here so he can separate you from your friends. You're too weak. You're pathetic! You're not good enough. You've been removed from the group because you can't cut it. You're just a girl!*

Jessica opened her mouth to refute the words running through her head. She found herself choking on sand. She fought to say the words with her mouth shut. *This isn't right. This isn't right.* Jessica's thoughts strengthened. *This isn't right! What did the King say before I went through the portal? He said this is a rescue mission. So I must be on a special mission for the King—one only I can do. It doesn't matter if I am a girl. Maybe this mission needs a girl. Maybe it needs me! The King asked me to serve Him, and I AM GOING TO SERVE HIM! I don't believe the words going through my head. I have faith.* Jessica fought the thoughts of rejection even harder.

A random image flashed through her mind, disrupting the battle raging inside her. A single word—*armor*—caught her by surprise, and she hesitated for a moment. *Armor* came through again. She placed her hand on her waist, and suddenly a belt appeared and grew wider, straightening and supporting her spine. She still heard the voices over and over telling her she wasn't good enough, that she wasn't going to make it. She began to speak aloud. This time the sand didn't seem to lodge in her mouth as much. "I said I don't believe you. I know the truth. I will not listen." Then she placed her hand on the side of her head and screamed, "I will put on my helmet! I will believe who I am!" A helmet suddenly appeared, layer upon layer unfolding about her head. She could no longer hear the tormentors through the helmet. Instead, she began hearing words such as "You are worthy! You are mine! I love you! You are a daughter of the King!" When Jessica heard these words, she remembered what the King had told her and rested her hand on her chest, feeling the broach—the Breastplate—her mother had given her. It grew and unfolded to engulf her in an iridescent sheath. It expanded, covering her chest, becoming a breastplate of protection. She was going to be okay. Her King was there for her. He had given her the resources she needed to move forward and not be demoralized.

When Jessica looked up, she saw a different world around her. The sand was no longer calm but swirling about her, buffeting her armor, pushing her from one side to the other, beating her, and trying to pull her down into the fray. Wind whipped around her with tornadic strength. She couldn't see through the swirling fog and debris. She tried to stand back up but found she couldn't. How did this come up so suddenly, or had it? Maybe it had always been there, unseen in the natural but there in this dimension. Yet this felt more real than the peaceful desert of just moments before. *This explains the sand in my mouth,* she thought to herself.

Jessica looked at the storm through her helmet's faceplate. She thought she saw something in the hot, sand-filled wind.

A hand flew by and then an arm and what could have been the top of a head—flat, hairless, and wrinkled. She could see figures racing, flying, and running through the sand. Spiders, lizards, and long-armed gangly things were all screeching and screaming, but she could no longer understand what they were saying. Her heart thumped in her chest. A scaly hand reached for her, and she pulled her arm back from it, letting it retreat into the swirling cloud of sand.

Thoughts quickly turned from *How did I get here?* to *How do I get out of here?* Jessica reached for the cord of her earbuds and started to yank them from her ears. Then she thought she might not be able to find the doorway without them. She had to stay in this dimension to see its doorways or portals of escape. She also knew she could not be here by chance. She had been selected for a mission; the others had not. This mission was one only she could complete. The King had total trust in her, and she was not going to let him down. Even so, was she really ready for this task? Her first move would require her to overcome the fear swirling around her. Much like the sandstorm before her, she would have to discern the importance of her travel here.

As she stood and came to her feet, the wind no longer buffeted her. The sand continued to swirl about her just outside her reach in every direction as though she was surrounded by an invisible force field. The creatures reaching through the sand couldn't get close enough to touch her, let alone grab her. She was safe if she didn't move, but stagnation solved nothing.

Jessica spoke. "Can anyone hear me?"

A soft voice answered her. "Yes, I hear you."

Jessica said, "I can't move."

The voice told her, "Look at your feet. Pick up one foot, and then pick up the other." As she did, she found boots on her feet that seemed to lift off the ground and hover in the sandstorm. She could hardly believe it. Here she was standing in the middle of a sandstorm, and it was like it wasn't even there.

Images were vague, and she dared not touch anything. She could hear distant, indistinct voices of hateful hissing creatures outside her bubble saying, "You can't do it. You're not strong enough. You're not ready for anything. You don't know what you're doing. He made a mistake trusting you. You don't even know what to do next."

She could see the creatures, but when they came at her, something buffeted them away. They had no effect on her. She knew it was because she believed what she heard, the truth from her belt and her helmet telling her she was a daughter of the King and that she deserved this mission and was worthy. She didn't know why she was there, but she knew she had to find out.

Sinister laughter sang behind the creepy voices. Some were louder than others, but each one cut her to the core. She thought she heard her grandfather's voice saying, "You're a girl. What can you do?"

Her mother's face appeared on the translucent screen before her and said, "Remember, when in doubt look to the truth. Think on the King's book, and find his truth." The words fell softly on Jessica's ears, and she realized they were coming through her helmet.

She reached for the belt around her waist. What had her mother called it? The Belt of Truth. However, she didn't feel the cloth belt her mother had given her. Instead, she felt a strong, metal girdle decorated with gems and stones. As she touched one of the stones, she began to hear her mother's voice reading from the book that had rested on her nightstand. "Be strong, and believe the King. He knows what you are going through. He is with you and will protect you." From another stone she heard, "The King sends his servant to guide you and show you the way, taking one step at a time."

"Okay," Jessica spoke aloud. "Show me what I need to see." As she stepped forward through the sand, she waited to see if something would show her which direction to go. The shoes seemed to send her forward. In the distance, she saw a building that was three stories high. It was made of brick and stone, and covered a large area. Grand double doors stood beneath arched stonework. Windows stretched on either side. It looked familiar to Jessica, but she was unsure where she had seen it. Attached to the top of the building were odd structures that didn't look like part of the original structure. They reminded her of gargoyles, and they seemed to move slightly.

As she stood, a dim, blue light shown upon a narrow path in front of her, and the bubble around her pushed through the haze. Strange body parts continued swirling around her. The word *choose* broke through her brain, and she had to agree. At one point, the path split to the left, revealing the front of the building. To the right she could see around the building. She stepped toward the left but found herself at the edge of the bubble with no light before her. She was clearly moving down the wrong path—well, at least the wrong path in her mind. She pushed against the bubble to get it to move left, but it wouldn't budge. At one point during her struggles, her foot broke through the edge of the bubble, and something tugged at her boot. She quickly yanked her foot back. It was clear that this path would be without the bubble's protection.

Resigned, she moved to the right, past the big doors, slowly staying within the bubble and watching for course changes. A small structure loomed before her. She was greeted with a horrible stench of garbage, which turned her stomach. *Why are smells so intense in this dimension?* Jessica grimaced. The blue light led her to the other side of the structure where a small, tiny object leaned against a brick wall.

As she moved closer, she could make out a form. It wasn't one of the gangly creatures swirling around. It was seated and experiencing the wrath of the wind. The creature seemed to be losing strength. It crumpled forward. As Jessica walked closer, she saw the distinct outline of two small creatures clinging to the small, frail body, whispering in its ears, "Do it. Go ahead. Nobody cares. Just end it. Who would even notice?" Then they cackled with a laugh that would have melted Dorothy's Wicked Witch of the West. Jessica shivered. She approached the figure and found a young girl around her age who was crying. The words the creatures spoke to the girl exposed their intent. A glass shard glistened in the girl's hand, ready to inflict damage.

Jessica stooped down to see the young girl's face, only to find Samantha Harris looking back. Jessica halted and looked away as Samantha's earlier stinging words surfaced in her mind. Then she thought, *Why did the King bring me to this place? Why did he want me to help this girl? Why, after all the pain inflicted by her?* For a moment, Jessica wanted her nemesis to finish the deed. Samantha deserved it, didn't she? Jessica spoke only one word—"Why?"

Samantha's soft voice seemed to respond. "Everyone hates me. My dad hates me. It's my fault she's gone." Samantha broke down. "I was the reason my sister was out that night."

As Jessica looked down at Samantha, only thoughts of sorrow and pity were in her mind. Jessica reached out to her, and her hand passed through Samantha. Startled, Jessica wasn't sure what to do, so she spoke. "Hey, I'm here. What can I do for you?"

Samantha pulled back and stammered. "I . . . I . . . I . . . Who are you? How did you get here? How did you find me? No one knows I'm here. No one cares I am here. I want to end the pain. I want it to go away." Samantha was now crying harder.

Samantha suddenly leaned back and looked at Jessica. Her face was contorted with anger. Her voice was low and deep. "I see you," said the voice. "And I know you. Get away from Samantha, you goody-two-shoes busybody. You can't save her. Get out of here."

A strange face undulated and seemed to faze in and out of Samantha's, but the anger remained distinct. "You can't stop her," it said. "She's already agreed. She's mine now and forever."

Jessica didn't know what came over her as she pointed her finger toward Samantha. "If she's decided, then why is she hesitating?" Jessica yelled. "You get away from her, and leave my friend alone!"

The creature laughed. "She has no friends. You don't care. She tormented you."

Jessica took a deep breath and calmed herself. Then she asked, "Who are you?"

The creature replied, "We are Hatred and Self-Loathing. Who are you?"

Jessica did not respond to the question but asked the creature, "And what is her name"?

"She is ours!" he replied. "She bears our name only." He snarled at Jessica. "You have still not told me your name."

Jessica smiled, for now she remembered the words her mother and father had told her—words she thought were strange and stupid but now made sense. Jessica said, "No, her name is Samantha, and I know because I am her friend. I have been sent by the King for I am his child, and I carry his authority."

"The King has forgotten this one and has chosen her to die," sneered the pitiful creature.

Jessica smiled and shook her head, "You speak only lies. The King does not wish for any to be lost but rather to choose life. You do not have permission to take that choice away from her. Get! Get out now! Leave her, and take your accomplices with you. By the authority of the King, you are hereby evicted. Return to your home dimension now!"

The creature screamed and flew off, followed by others who were with it. The sandstorm calmed, and only a soft misty rain remained. Jessica ran to Samantha, who dropped the broken piece of glass from her hand. Jessica kicked it away.

When Jessica squatted down in front of Samantha, she looked up at her. Now Jessica understood why she was here. But she wasn't sure why the King had sent her to this person. Jessica stared at Samantha and wondered why Samantha was not tormenting her with her usual cruel words. In her helmet, Jessica heard the word *forgiveness*. In her mind's eye, she saw a broken heart being healed.

"Is this Samantha's heart?" Jessica asked the voice in her helmet.

"No, it is yours" came the reply in her ears.

As Jessica reached out to Samantha, her hand again passed through the girl sitting before her. "What's your name?"

"Samantha. Who are you? Why can't I see you?" Tears streamed down Samantha's face as she responded to the person she couldn't see. "I don't want to die. But I don't want to live either."

Jessica answered, "You must want to live. Life is not easy, but there are those who want to help you, even if you have behaved cruelly toward them. They still want to help you." Jessica sighed. "I don't know why, but I was sent here for you." Jessica swallowed and continued. "Just know you are loved. The King loves you. You don't want to end everything. There is so much you can do to help others if you'll just let him love you."

Slowly, Samantha stood up. She didn't understand what was so compelling about this simple message of love, but she wanted to know more. Samantha replied, "How can you love me? You don't know me."

Jessica responded, "I know that the King loves you. You have been stolen and taken from him. He wants you back. He sent me to find you and bring you back—back to the kingdom and to his loving arms."

Samantha snickered. "You're crazy."

"Maybe, but it could be worth a shot," Jessica replied. "Can it be worse than where you are now?" Jessica looked around at a soft, swirling mist no longer beating against the two girls.

Samantha said, "I want that. I want protection. I want to feel that someone cares."

In her helmet, Jessica heard these words: "Take her hand." So Jessica reached out her hand and said, "Reach out and put your hand in mine. Trust me, and we will get out of this together." Jessica wasn't sure this would work, but it was worth a try.

Samantha reached out her hand and placed it in Jessica's. The creatures still around them began to writhe, scream, and shout. They behaved as though they were in pain. They were furious when Samantha took Jessica's hand in faith and no longer believed their lies. The sandstorm suddenly stopped. Samantha stood up and began to move toward Jessica. "What is that?" Samantha asked.

When Jessica looked up to see what Samantha was referring to, she saw a door only a few feet away. Jessica knew what to do. Quickly she pulled on Samantha's hand and said, "We have to go."

Samantha hesitated. "I don't know."

Jessica replied, "We can only do this if you're willing. I can't make you come with me. You must choose."

Samantha stopped and looked toward the door and the light coming from it. "Okay. I choose to go with you." She stepped forward with Jessica. The door opened, and both girls stepped through the opening.

CHAPTER 12

The Lost Base

Daniel was hit with a blast of icy wind and dropped to his knees when he walked through the doorway. He wrapped his arms around himself and closed his eyes. *Why does this keep happening? How am I supposed to survive this?*

Daniel felt a touch on his arm as Gabriella whispered in his ear barely louder than the wind whipping around him. "Daniel, come with me. I can get you out of this storm and somewhere safe." Daniel didn't speak but simply allowed her to help him to his feet and lead him through the wind and cold.

After a few minutes and a few missteps, they were in a cave and protected. "I came through right behind you and saw you fall," Gabriella added softly.

Daniel looked at Gabriella and the coat she was wearing. He said, "So where is my coat? It's freezing here." Daniel realized he was shaking from the cold.

"Here." Gabriella pulled a small, six-inch cube from a backpack she was carrying and handed it to Daniel.

Daniel stared at the small cube for only a moment before opening it. When he pulled on the piece of fabric inside, it seemed to come out of a black hole, revealing a thick, warm jacket just his size. Daniel smiled. "I don't know why everything here still surprises me," and then he laughed at the mystery of the box.

Putting on the jacket, Daniel felt much warmer. He smiled as he rubbed the sleeves of his new coat. "It's even my favorite color," he exclaimed.

"Your favorite color is black?" Gabriella questioned and then looked down at the multi-tonal pink and purple coat she was wearing. "I always thought the color represented a rank, but now that you mention it, this is my favorite color." Gabriella rubbed her coat. "The King is amazing," she whispered to herself.

Daniel smiled at Gabriella and looked up at the cave around them. "What do we do now?"

"Well, the King sent me here to find an ally base we have lost contact with. You were sent here to help me." Gabriella paused a moment. "At least I can only imagine and hope that this is why you are here."

"Samuel said my friends were in danger. I thought I was coming to rescue them." Daniel said.

"Well, for whatever reason, you are here. The King must have a plan," Gabriella reasoned. "In the meantime, you can help me find the lost base. Perhaps your friends are there." Gabriella stopped looking around the frozen cave walls and looked intently at Daniel. "Was there anything you were looking for before you left Samuel? Perhaps that has something to do with why you are here."

Daniel turned to look at Gabriella. "Well, Samuel mentioned my armor. Could that be it?"

"Anything is possible with our King." Gabriella smiled at Daniel. "I wonder..." She moved to investigate the ice walls that formed the cave around them. "I wonder if there is anything buried within the layers." Gabriella ran her hands over a large section of the ice. It seemed to melt the ice slightly, removing the frost that covered it. In the shadows beneath her hand, Daniel thought he saw something.

Daniel stopped Gabriella. "What is that?" he said, pointing to the warmed ice.

"I'm not sure," replied Gabriella. "What can we use to break the ice? Look around, and see if there is anything here." Both began searching the cave to find something to use.

"Look here!" exclaimed Daniel from the back side of the ice cave. "Someone has left a pickaxe and a hatchet. Let's use them." Daniel picked up the tools and handed one to Gabriella. Both began chipping at the ice wall. The ice seemed to break away easily for Daniel and Gabriella until they hit a large, metal-clad trunk. They continued to chip away around the metal box, being careful not to damage it.

The trunk moved slightly forward out of the ice. Daniel grabbed the handle on the side and pulled while Gabriella continued to chip the ice around it. Finally, it gave way, and Daniel sat down as the ice released the box. It slid across the icy floor, coming to a halt when it collided with Daniel's outstretched legs.

Daniel ran his hand over the cold, icy surface of the trunk.

Metal straps inlaid with jewels of every color wrapped around the trunk, holding the metal plating. It was beautiful, unlike the boxes his father and Gigi had their armor in. This box appeared large enough to hold a real set of armor. While Daniel continued running his hand along the metal, he found no keyhole. Only a small disc-shaped surface was visible where a key might have been inserted.

"Daniel, place your thumb on that round metal plate. Perhaps it was made for you!" Gabriella exclaimed excitedly.

"How would they have my biometrics?" Daniel questioned Gabriella.

"The King has whatever we need. Try it. See what good things he provides." Gabriella was so excited that she was beginning to bounce.

Daniel placed his thumb on the plate, heard a faint click, and felt the lock disengage. His hands shook as he placed them on either side of the lid, slowly lifting it. The trunk appeared to be empty. Daniel slowly lifted himself to his knees for a clearer view of the contents. There were only five small items on the bottom of the box—a wide strip of cloth, what appeared to be a small metal stick, a round pair of silver discs, a name badge engraved with the word *MINE*, and what looked like an earbud. "What is this supposed to be?" asked Daniel. Gabriella's bouncing had morphed into an energetic dance.

"You found it! You found it! You found it!" she kept repeating over and over.

"What have I found? It looks like more junk, just like my dad's box and Gigi's box. It doesn't make sense. What is this

The Lost Base

stuff? And why does the King want me to have it? How can this help me find my friends or even your missing base of operation?" Daniel sat back and watched Gabriella continue dancing. "Gabriella, help me understand this! You're supposed to be my guide! Guide me!" Daniel stood up and reached out for her shoulders to get her to stop dancing and singing.

"What?" Gabriella's response was loud enough to echo throughout the ice cave. They both looked around in surprise and then stared down a tunnel that had formed on the back wall of the cave.

Daniel grabbed Gabriella's shoulders more tightly and pulled her attention back to him. "I don't know what to do with these things. How is this supposed to be armor? None of this makes sense to me. What do I do? What was the King thinking? Please help me."

Gabriella spoke as she looked back at Daniel. She was much calmer now. "Please do not lose the importance of your armor. It is a gift for you. It is activated by the King's very Spirit to ensure victory. The pieces work together to support and protect you. This box only holds a representation of each piece. Let me show you."

Gabriella reached into the box and retrieved the wide cloth. "Wrap this around your waist. It is the Belt of Truth." She handed the cloth to Daniel, who wrapped it awkwardly around his waist, unsure of how to do it. Gabriella continued instructing Daniel. "It doesn't matter. You don't have to be exact. It knows what to do." Daniel relaxed, and the cloth seemed to wrap itself around his waist, stretching and expanding to fit snuggly.

"Perfect!" exclaimed Gabriella. "When you wear the belt, it engulfs you in truth like a force field. Truth grounds us. It does not change and cannot be found in the things that change. Truth also does not come from experience. The source of truth can only be found in the words of the King. Following them keeps the belt activated."

Gabriella continued. "The wearer sees things as the King sees them, giving a revelation of reality. Truth exposes deception and separates fact from fiction. It defines our sense of good and evil and calls for a choice of who we will be. If you don't know the truth, how will you know what is good and what is evil?"

Gabriella paused a minute and then stood up. She touched his belt and added, "Knowing the truth of and about the King is critical." Gabriella looked up at Daniel. "When we are weak in our convictions, truth grounds us. It is the only thing we can use to reject evil. The Dragon is the primary illusionist. He makes evil appealing and goodness boring. Rightful truth is based on the words of the King. It is the only thing we can use to reject the Dragon."

When Daniel looked up, he wondered how he would see the world differently. He then reached into the trunk, picked up a badge, and held it up to Gabriella. "What does this do? Why does it say *MINE*?"

"It says you no longer belong to the Darkness; you belong to the Light, to the King. It says you are in right standing with the Forces of the Light." Gabriella stood at the entrance of the ice cave and looked out at the storm beyond. "The truth is that the battle has already been won. The Dragon is defeated. Those who allow him to dominate give him a legal right to your world. The King defeated the Darkness and is trying to bring your people out from it, but they must *want* to follow the King in order to be free."

Gabriella turned back to face Daniel. "This badge says you have the right to be a part of the world outside the Darkness. It gives you the authority to speak on behalf of the King. It also covers who you are and gives you the identity of the King to those of this world. Touch it, and see what happens."

Daniel pressed lightly on the badge, and it began to expand to cover his chest with a light blue breastplate. Gabriella formed a snowball from the ice on the floor and threw it at Daniel. It hit the breastplate and broke apart. Daniel raised his hand to strike himself in the chest and managed to do exactly that. "Ow!" The breastplate allowed his hand to go through it as though nothing was there. "Wow! I could have used this at school when I faced Justin Collins."

Gabriella smiled. "It takes a lot of practice to bring the armor into your world and make it work. You may get there. We will have to see." She then turned back to the box and extended her hand toward it. "There are more items for you here."

Inside, Daniel found a pair of boots and what looked like a pen. He sat on the floor and noticed that the ice no longer bothered him. He put on the boots and stood up. "Do these have a name?" he asked Gabriella.

"Yes. They are Shoes of Peace," she replied as she began searching the cave.

"Yeah, I can kick the tar out of my enemy and bring peace." Daniel kicked into the air, and Gabriella snickered.

"Not exactly," she replied. "They are for the exact opposite. They are not offensive but defensive. They help you stand firm and give you courage in the battle."

"In the midst of a battle," added Daniel.

Gabriella turned to face him and said, "Anytime, not just in a battle. Now we need to get going. We can't just stay here. Put the final two objects into your pocket, and we will discuss them later. Let's go. Trouble is coming for us."

Gabriella tapped the sides of Daniel's boots, and they automatically tightened around his legs. Daniel carefully stood up and stomped on the ground. He felt cleats appear on the bottom of his boots. "I'm ready," he said. He looked up at Gabriella, pursed his lips, and shoved the pen and earbud into his pocket.

Gabriella stood at an opening in the wall of the cave. It was the farthest distance from the entrance where they had come in. She opened her hand, which held a small, round device. It was a crystal ball emitting a blue light that reflected off the walls of ice. Together they walked forward through the tunnel of ice.

Daniel had been watching Gabriella and her blue light when something caught his attention. "What is that?" he asked, stopping and pointing to the ice wall beside them.

Gabriella touched the ice with her hand and wiped off the fog, which revealed a strange sight. Encased beneath the ice was a battle frozen in time. People of various ages and attire were battling strange creatures nearly twice as tall as they were. The people held hatchets and ice picks as battle weapons. They didn't appear to be successful in the battle against the giants, who appeared to be some form of space aliens. The people were losing the battle. Several were on the ground in great pain or dying. Daniel turned to look at Gabriella. "What does this mean? Should we release them or leave them?"

Gabriella placed her hand on Daniel's outstretched arm. "Leave them. Remember, I told you the battle is already won. They did not believe it and continued to fight. They will fail, but this will keep them safe until they can be convinced. In this world they are not harmed. In yours, there is much damage because they are not using the weapons of the King but rather weapons of their own making. We must leave this problem to the King."

When Daniel took a step away from the wall to see more, he heard a faint cracking sound. "What is that sound?" he asked.

"Do not move, Daniel. It is the enemy's trap." Gabriella slowly turned and stretched her hand with the blue light toward Daniel. The ice beneath him was clear, thin, and full of cracks.

Daniel took in a deep breath and looked at the ice. *What could he do? What if the ice broke?* "I've been wondering when I would be going home. I never thought the question would be *if* I was going home." He turned and looked back at Gabriella.

"Do not fear the enemy's tricks. Remember to gain strength from your shoes of peace. What do you need them to do to stop the fear?" asked Gabriella.

"I need them to make the ice stronger, move me past the trap, or reverse time and keep me from walking out on this patch of ice altogether. What do you want me to say?" Daniel was now raising his voice.

"Well, the first thing you can do is stop panicking. That's exactly what the Darkness wants you to do. The second is to not say . . ."

Daniel interrupted. "Calm down? Don't panic? Too late. I am panicking!" At that moment the ice beneath Daniel gave way, and he began falling into what seemed like a bottomless pit. Then strong arms reached under his own and began to lift him upward. He could neither see nor feel anything around him, but he was rising.

In his ear he heard, "Put your earbud in." Floating beside the smooth ice wall, Daniel reached into his pocket, removed the earbud, and placed it in his ear. "There. Now you can hear me," the voice said.

"Who is this?" Daniel asked.

"I couldn't let you fall. I love you too much. You're mine. Remember? I am always with you. You never have to be afraid. Together we can do anything. The shoes are there to remind you of that."

Daniel thought for a moment. "What do I do? Click my heels together three times to make me fly?"

There was a bit of humor now in the voice in the earbud. "If that helps you to believe in my power, go ahead. Whatever it takes. Give it a try."

Daniel looked toward his new boots, careful not to look all

The Lost Base

the way down. He clicked his heels together three times and said, "I'm not in Kansas anymore."

The voice laughed aloud. "I didn't mean to say that! Just say, 'I believe the King and his power is limitless.'"

Daniel repeated the words and felt himself lift upward. The arms around him vanished. He continued to rise along the ice wall until he was level with Gabriella again. Then he stepped forward to the cave floor where she was standing. Gabriella just stood smiling at him. Then she grabbed his hand, and they continued their journey through the ice tunnel.

Within a few minutes, they came upon a set of double metal doors. The handle was icy cold, and it was difficult to engage the latch. Daniel laid his hands on the frozen latch and said, "I choose to use the glory of the King to melt the lock and latch of this door, to release it for the purpose of the King." Daniel's hands became warm as he held the door handle. After a minute or two, Daniel tried the latch again, and the door opened easily. Together, Daniel and Gabriella walked through the large double doors and into the base.

Inside, the base was dark with only dim lighting on the ceiling. The carpet on the floor was dirty, and the walls were peeling. On the wall, Daniel saw a plaque.

....

While you have the Light, believe in the Light that you may become Sons and Daughters of the Light.

....

As Daniel looked down the hall, trying to see what was at the other end, he saw a small, fiery light. It began to grow slowly. Daniel asked Gabriella, "What is that?"

Gabriella squinted to see down the hall. "I don't know, but it looks like it is getting larger."

Daniel sank to the floor, "It's coming right at us." He waited for the light to arrive.

Gabriella smiled. "No, it is something else. Come on. Follow me."

CHAPTER 13

Caleb joins the Journey

"Once upon a time..."

"Oh, Daddy," whispered Beth, "it's going to be one of those stories." With wide eyes and a small, slight quiver, the four-year-old settled down a little farther beneath her bed covers. The sheet and blanket cocooned her tiny body, making any movement unlikely.

Across the small, pink room, Julie lay in a white spindle twin bed, a match to the one Beth was cocooned in. The sheet and blanket spread across the bed up to the headboard. Bumps hinted at the young child beneath. Long, slender limbs reached for the headboard, and the top edge of the covers rotated up and down to the seven-year-old's sides, exposing her face and arms to the cool air. "Yuk! Not another one of those stories." Her voice dropped to a deep tone with each word, resting a bit on the extended *those*.

Daddy smiled. "Now, Julie." He purposely kept his tone soft and gentle. "You know your sister loves a good once-upon-a-time story. I remember when another young lady loved them as well." Daddy sat in a white, straight-backed rocking chair between the two girls' beds.

Julie sat up straight as a small white cat fell to the floor beside her bed. "Dad, I'm too old for that. I like real stories, not little girly fairy tales." Julie's arms waved in great circles, knocking another stuffed animal onto the floor.

"Really?" Daddy replied curiously, looking at the stuffed animals on the floor and then on the bed. His gaze followed up the wall to three long shelves positioned carefully above Julie's head. A lone fuzzy turtle sat on the lowest shelf. He could still hear little Julie's voice. "But Daddy, I don't have room for all my babies on this little bed." The move and the sacrifices associated with the move had been especially difficult for his oldest daughter.

Julie lay back down, making it difficult for her daddy, Caleb, to find her beneath the pile of "babies" on the bed. A long arm reached up into the air and over the edge of the bed, followed by shoulders and a head. Long, blond hair swung down and brushed the floor as the little "pretzel" snatched the cat and the bear, swung back up, and disappeared into the mound of animals. "Besides," came a voice from the pile of animals, softer and more mature, "Mom says it's time to grow up and be more responsible."

They all sat in silence for a moment until Beth softly asked, "Daddy, can we be more responsible tomorrow and hear the story tonight?"

Caleb joins the Journey

Caleb smiled and answered, "Yes, Little Bug, we can do that. Is that all right with you, Julie?"

"Yes, Daddy, that would be all right," she answered, barely audible.

Turning back to Beth, Caleb began again. "Once upon a time, there lived a little prince, and his name was Caleb. This little prince didn't live in a castle. He lived . . ."

Julie sat up in her bed, spilling almost all her animals. "Really, Daddy? Who is this little prince named Caleb?" Julie stared at her dad with her head tilted to one side and her eyebrows raised.

"I know who Caleb is," exclaimed Beth.

"You do?" Caleb asked playfully. "Who is he?"

"He's the prince that comes to my room every night and plays with me," Beth spoke with glee.

Julie and Caleb looked at each other. Then Caleb asked slowly, "How does he come to you, and what kind of games do you play?"

"In my dreams," Beth answered matter-of-factly.

"Oh," Caleb replied and looked at Julie. Both smiled at each other.

Later that night, Caleb peeked into the girls' room to check on them. A blue, glowing knight stood beside Beth's bed. Caleb stepped just inside the door and closed it silently behind him. Julie was snoring softly, but Beth was not in her bed.

"Where is my daughter?" Caleb quietly growled at the knight.

"She is playing with the other children. Would you like to see?" the knight quietly responded.

"Who are you, and why are you here?" Caleb continued his defensive stance.

"Let me show you. I am not here to harm you or your family. I came to find you. Please come with me and let me show you what you have forgotten." The knight stretched out his hand to Caleb. He wasn't sure why he accepted it, but he did. Suddenly, a circle of fire and sparks appeared to grow large enough for them to pass through. Together they stepped through to a sunny, grassy landscape with children playing. One of the children was Beth.

Caleb started to walk toward Beth, but the knight held out his hand to stop him. The knight spoke to Caleb. "Let her play. I need your help. I have a mission for you. Will you help?"

Caleb felt a whisper in his heart. "Do it for her and all the other children."

Caleb continued to watch Beth and the other children as he answered the whisper in his heart. "Okay, I will." When Caleb turned toward the knight, the knight was gone. Caleb also noticed that he wasn't on the grassy knoll either. Instead, he stood inside a small, dimly lit room. Caleb turned around to find what appeared to be several teenagers sitting in a circle of chairs. They were all facing a young man who was seated in front of a small table where a large book sat open. Caleb stood, staring at the kids, and they sat staring back at him. Then they all turned toward an approaching small, blue light coming down the hall toward the kids and Caleb.

The blue light began to illuminate the room as Daniel and Gabriella joined the small group. Gabriella closed her hand, extinguishing the blue glow within it. Everyone stood up in silence for a few moments, and then the young man at the table with the book spoke first. "We have been asking for reinforcements. Has the King sent you?"

Daniel answered, "He has. My name is Daniel, and this is my guide, Gabriella."

This was followed by several teenagers saying, "Hi, Daniel" and "Hi, Gabriella."

The young man at the table continued. "My name is Michael. This is my sister, Lilly, and Mark, James, John, Maria, Mathew, Luke, Rachel, Amanda, Stephen, and Petra. We all live here on the base."

Daniel said to the kids, "It's so dark. What happened here? Where are the lights?"

Michael added, "The lights have been growing dim for some time now. I need to know if you are here to help us."

"Yes, we are," responded Gabriella. "Command lost communication with the base, and I was sent here with Daniel to see why."

Everyone looked at Caleb, who just shrugged. "I'm Caleb, I was also sent by the King, but I'm not sure what my mission is. I'm sure we'll figure it out at some point." Caleb smiled at the kids, and they smiled back.

They all turned to look at Michael who spoke next. "I was cleaning a closet, and I found this book. It looks like a training manual and historical documentation about the King. If it is, we are fighting this war all wrong," he added. "And If I am reading this right, the war is over."

Caleb asked, "What war are you fighting, and what did you find in the manual that makes you think things aren't right here?"

Michael answered, "It's the war between the Light of Love and the Darkness of Evil. We've been fighting the war all my life, as have my parents and grandparents. If the war is over, why are we still fighting? Why has the King left us here to continue the fight? Why has he not removed the Darkness so we can live in peace? It makes me wonder if any of this is real." Michael stopped and looked at the newcomers.

Caleb answered before the others could. "First, Michael, I believe the King is real because I just spoke with him, and he sent me here. As for your other questions, they all have the same answer. Often, at the end of a war, many of the troops don't know the war is over or they choose not to believe it. So troops must be sent out to capture them and bring them the truth and often justice."

"And we are those troops?" asked Michael.

"I would believe that to be so," said Caleb.

Gabriella spoke. "The base has been infiltrated by the enemy."

Caleb interrupted. "There are often many who devote themselves to the teaching of the Darkness. They fool the people around them and lead them away from the teachings of the King."

Gabriella continued. "There are a few of those here who are allowing the Darkness to block communications with the forces of the King. I was sent to help you discover the cause and find a way to fix it."

Caleb joins the Journey

"Okay," said Michael. "Where do we start?"

Gabriella said, "The Darkness will always set up a position of strength to work from. It could be an actual structure, a little habitat for a creature of the Darkness. From there, the creature will influence the thinking of others. Do you know where there might be one of those on the base?"

Lilly, sitting next to Michael, was the youngest of the group and appeared to be about 12 years old. She stood up and said, "I think I might know where the stronghold could be. We will have to get past the Lieutenant Commander's assembly to reach it."

"The next thing we need to do is figure out who may have given the creature of Darkness its right to be here," said Gabriella. "They have no rights except those the final creature gives them."

Caleb moved toward the hallway. "We need to find the Commander and see what he knows."

Michael stood up and moved toward Caleb. "The Commander has been missing for some time. The Lieutenant Commander is leading the assembly in his place. They never leave the assembly. They never go into battle. They only encourage new recruits, always recruiting."

"Come on," added Daniel, "we need to see what they are doing."

Together the group moved down the dark hallway where Gabriella and Daniel had come from. Down the hallway, they entered a large room Michael called the Greeting Room where most entered the base. "When we came through, this room was empty," Daniel offered, pointing across the Greeting Room, "We came through the doors at the opposite end of this hallway." To their left were the main doors to the building. Directly across from the main doors was the Assembly Room. It was separated from the Greeting Room by several sets of double doors. In the Greeting Room, tables were set up with drinks and snacks. Michael told Caleb, Daniel, and Gabriella, "They do this for the new recruits. There are always new ones coming in. Very few leave."

Caleb turned toward the Assembly Room doors. "Let's see what is going on in there." All agreed and headed toward the doors.

Inside, the room was dark. The crowd inside was watching a performance on a stage opposite the doors. Many stared at the event taking place, and few blinked. "In my world, that indicates they have stopped listening," Caleb whispered. The others nodded.

Michael pointed to those sitting closest to the aisle where they had entered. "Look, they have been chained to their chairs."

Daniel pointed to their necks. "Those keys around their necks will most likely unlock their chains, but they probably don't know it."

Michael asked, "How do you know that?"

"I've seen this before," Daniel responded softly. "It happened to a friend of mine."

Scattered throughout the audience were a few who were shouting and raising their arms in reaction to the program

Caleb joins the Journey

on the stage. As Lieutenant Commander Robertson barked orders at the crowd, various scantily clad young girls danced to exciting music led by an exotically dressed older woman.

Michael pointed to the woman leading the girls. "She showed up shortly after the Commander disappeared."

Many parents were taking their children to the front to be placed on the edge of the stage. Suddenly, a dark-clad creature ran from the curtains along the back of the platform to the front and pushed one of the little children off the stage. The crowd erupted and then returned to their earlier states as the Lieutenant Commander continued. Gabriella turned her head and began to cry. Daniel took hold of her shoulders and led her out of the Assembly Room. Caleb and the others followed.

Outside, the doors closed behind the group. In front of them, the tables were crowded with people. "Newcomers," Michael said softly, looking across the large room.

Caleb told Michael and the other kids, "Send them home." With his voice trailing off, Caleb said, "There is nothing here for them today." Then he added more sternly, "I have seen this before. Send them home. It isn't safe for them here."

The others looked at Caleb in silence. Gabriella shook her head and placed her hand on Caleb's back. "I am so sorry," she whispered. Daniel wondered what she was thinking. What did she know?

Suddenly, Caleb began swinging his arms and screaming loudly. "Get out! Get out! Get out of here! It's a trap! Get out! Find your peace somewhere else! Not here! Not today!"

Daniel looked at Gabriella as she nodded. "Yeah, not today." Daniel began shouting. "Come back tomorrow. It'll be a better show to see. The show is closed for today. There's been a . . . a . . . malfunction."

The others accepted the call and began chasing the people across the Greeting Room and out the main doors. Then they closed and locked the doors behind the people.

When they turned to face the Assembly Room, an elderly woman stood before them. Her grey hair was a mass of tangles, her dress was tattered, and her face had several skin tags and moles. "What are you doing?" the witch asked.

Gabriella walked around the woman and began poking at her. Each time Gabriella poked, the woman jumped, looked around, but said nothing. Gabriella returned to Daniel's side. "It is as I thought. She can't see me."

Daniel's face scrunched. "What do you mean?" he asked.

The woman put her hands on her hips and said gruffly, "What do I mean? I mean to stop your horsing around and get this base back on track, to add to our recruits. There's a battle coming, and we mean to win it. Now what do you mean, young man?"

Caleb addressed the woman in a gentle tone. "Ma'am, what is your name?"

"I don't know what it matters to you, but my name is Agatha," she replied harshly.

Caleb continued. "Perhaps you can help us talk to the Commander after the performance. We have an important issue to discuss with him as soon as he is available. It is of utmost importance in the success of the war. Can you take care of that, please?"

"Yes, yes I can," Agatha replied in a much calmer voice as she headed to the Assembly Room.

Daniel looked at Caleb quizzically. "How did you know that would work?"

Caleb smiled. "Because she felt she was important, so I used that to our advantage."

"Is she?" Daniel asked.

"I doubt it," replied Caleb.

"She's not," Michael added with a sneer.

"So now I have a question for each of you kids," Caleb said as he turned to the group that had been following Michael. "How many of you can see our friend Gabriella?" Nine of the twelve followers of Michael raised their hands. The last three did so slowly. "It is very important that you are honest about this. Your lives could be in danger if you are not truthful." Three hands went down. "Okay. Good. We can do something about that."

Michael questioned Caleb. "What does it mean if they can't see her?"

Caleb turned to Michael. "How old does she look to you, Michael?"

"I would guess she is about five or six. Why?" Michael questioned.

Caleb continued. "Okay. Good. You're safe." Addressing the group, Caleb continued. "Gabriella is not from this dimension. Only those who have been enlightened can see and hear her. In my world, she would be called an angel. I must ask this to each of you. You have been reading the book, but have you committed to follow the King?" The same nine lifted their hands above their heads. "Great! Everyone else must stop their journey now. You may choose to make that commitment later if you stay here, but you can't go with us. It will be much too dangerous."

Lilly raised her hand and asked, "Why is she only five?"

Gabriella stomped her feet. "I am not only five! Haven't you ever heard of a cherub? They look like babies, but they are also very old."

Daniel smiled at the others who had raised their hands and were snickering. He glanced at Gabriella who remained indignant.

CHAPTER 14

Discovery

Caleb looked at the group and asked, "Who found the stronghold? We need to destroy it." Caleb smiled. "This is the dangerous part."

Lilly raised her hand again and replied, "I did. After my brother found the book, we all began searching the base for more answers. That's when I found a door with a lock on it that wasn't there before. My mother commented that she remembered a staircase to the resonator, but she didn't remember a door covering the staircase, and it never would have been locked."

"What's a resonator?" Daniel asked.

"It recreates sounds to open portals to the King," Rachel answered. "We were trying to imitate the resonator when you arrived. I didn't think we could produce the same sounds and get our message through, but Michael did."

"It looks like you were successful after all," replied Caleb, smiling. "Good job!" He held up his hand for a high five, and all the kids responded by holding up their own hands. Only Daniel slapped Caleb's hand. Caleb paused and added, "Okay then. Where's that door?"

The small crowd spread out, and Lilly led them to an almost invisible door near the entrance to the Assembly Room. There were several locks on the door. Caleb lowered his head and closed his eyes. A soft blue light fell upon him. It seemed to distract him for a moment. He reached into his pocket and pulled out a short, stick-like object. Daniel saw that it was like his own. Caleb smiled, exhaled quietly, and said to himself, *You are always a surprise—everything I need, just when I need it. You are Jireh.* The others watched as he jerked his hand, and the stick grew to a six-foot-long staff.

Agatha reappeared in front of the door, blocking Caleb. She said, "You cannot open this door. It is too dangerous. It was locked to protect the people. You cannot do this!"

Caleb leaned over the woman. He spoke directly into her face in a strong, quiet tone. "I am here on official business of the King. You cannot stop me. I have all authority to open this door, and we are going through it. Go to your Commander. Tell him the King, A'Primas, has sent his general."

The old woman screamed at the name and ran to tell the Lieutenant Commander.

Caleb turned back to the mysterious door and its various locks. He pointed his staff at each lock. A blue lightning bolt emitted from the staff, and each lock opened. When the last lock was released, Michael anxiously reached for the doorknob. Caleb stopped him and touched the knob with his staff. Sparks emitted from the staff to the knob. It glowed blue, and then the knob turned silver. Caleb turned to Michael and said, "Now you can touch it, Michael." Then he offered him the first look.

Michael slowly pushed the door inward to open it. The stairwell beyond was even darker than the hallways of the base. It reeked of an odor Michael had never smelled before. He heard Daniel's words coming from behind him—"It smells like burning sulfur."

Caleb replied, "The smell shows this is indeed the location of the stronghold. Be prepared for anything." They all held their positions.

After a moment, Caleb urged them on. "Time to move forward. Don't be afraid. Fear is their only real weapon. All other weapons come down to lies and what you are made to believe."

At that moment, Gabriella spoke up. "I cannot continue with you. I will wait here until you return."

Daniel stepped next to Gabriella. "Why not? You have come so far. What is wrong?"

Gabriella faced Daniel and softened her tone. "I don't have the authority to wage war here. This battle is for the final creature to take its authority and wield it."

One by one, Daniel and the others gave Gabriella a hug and bid her goodbye. Gabriella accepted the hugs and well wishes, and then she laughed. "You all act like you are going to your deaths. You are not! The King is with you always."

Everyone looked at Caleb who laughed heartily. "No, not me. I am not the King."

They looked back at Gabriella who continued. "The King is always watching, and he has given each of you a gift to fight this battle. Listen to Caleb. He was once a great general of the King's army. He will guide you to complete this mission. The King has already defeated Darkness. He needs you to reclaim your territory. Drive out the Darkness. Then I will see you. Remember, there is no fear when the King is near, and he is always near." Gabriella smiled at the group of young warriors.

Michael turned away from Gabriella and stepped into the stairwell. The others followed, with Daniel bringing up the rear. As Daniel stepped into the stairwell, he felt a distinct difference in the atmosphere. It was stuffier and hotter, somehow... different. He almost felt like he had passed through another portal. He paused and turned back to look at Gabriella, but he couldn't see her.

The carpet covering the steps was moist and squishy. The corners of the steps were crusted with filth and what looked like years of dirt and dust. At the first landing, Daniel noticed papers thrown about. They were covered with lines and funny looking dots with flags on them. Michael admitted that the images looked familiar to him, but he couldn't remember where he had seen them before. Caleb, standing next to Michael, stopped suddenly. Daniel looked up the stairs. They seemed to continue forever, getting darker as they went. Caleb raised his hand and placed it on the wall, closed his eyes, and lowered his head. Ornamental fixtures slowly came on and began illuminating their path.

As they climbed, Caleb began to talk to the others about the ways of the King. "The King is with us and protecting us. We must trust in him and his truth. You must believe what you have learned about the King and his ways. It will be as a belt of protection."

Daniel stopped suddenly. "Like a belt that protects your insides." Daniel opened his jacket to reveal the belt he had received from the trunk. The others came to his side to see and touch his belt.

Caleb smiled and continued. "Remember," Caleb tapped his chest, "you are worthy of the King's love and protection. Wear this knowledge like a breastplate. Remember who you are—a child of Love himself, a joint heir with the King. This is why Darkness hates you so much. Darkness will try to convince you that you are flawed and unworthy of the King's love. It is a lie."

They kept climbing more steps as Caleb continued to instruct them. "Darkness will try to destroy you. The truth not only tells us we are loved by the King but gives us peace, even courage. Think of this as shoes you wear, guiding your steps, because you are not afraid." The group stopped abruptly on their climb. Caleb turned to see why.

Lilly stood near the rear of the group. She looked at each of her fellow battle seekers, smiled, and then stomped her feet. "I am not afraid!" she shouted. Lilly's sandals transformed into beautiful, shiny, metal boots. When she stood to face the others, she was wearing a beautiful, embroidered belt.

Michael stepped down to look at his sister. "Lil! That's awesome!" Michael stood before Lilly and smiled at her. "Well, if you can be unafraid, then I can too." Michael looked down to see his own belt and boots. One by one they all did the same, building on the faith of the others. Looking around, they also noticed strong, gleaming, metal plates of armor covering their chests.

Caleb looked at each of them, telling them how wonderful their armor was. "But that is not all the King has for you." He continued his instruction. "Be sure to protect what you hear. Like a helmet that blocks the blows of the enemy, you must block the false words of Darkness and those who choose to befriend him. He will try to fill your head with untruths to make you forget what you have learned, destroy your plans, and finally kill you or your promises. Don't let that happen." Caleb continued to climb with the new King's warriors in tow. "Remember the words of the book. Speak the words, and use them like swords to defeat the lies of Darkness. Use them as a weapon. Finally, the King is listening. Talk to him always." Caleb stopped and turned to face the kids. "As you speak with him, remember your brothers and sisters." Caleb circled his right hand around to include the whole group. "Now, are you ready to continue to the top?"

They all nodded with determination on each of their faces. Caleb turned and continued the climb with the others in tow. Daniel and Michael brought up the rear.

On the landing at the top of the stairs, Caleb stopped to make sure everyone had caught up and were together. Turning to them, he spoke. "There is something we must do first." Ten people stood on the landing, the nine kids facing Caleb. "We must first be covered in the protection and grace of the King and Jireh, the Father." Caleb reached above his head and spoke out loud. "Oh, Great Father and our King, we ask you to fill these brave ones with your power and your grace for the battle ahead of us. Give us the wisdom to fight this battle for you and your kingdom." Then he lowered his arms and looked at the others as they were all illuminated by a soft, blue light. The faces that looked back at him were stiff and determined. Finally, he spoke. "Great King, go with us into the battle that is before us. Thank you for your presence."

Turning back to the door, Caleb placed his staff against it. The door took on a soft, blue glow and then turned pearly white and opened.

CHAPTER 15

The Resonator Room

Inside, the room was dark except for a few dim lights hanging on the wall. Although it was difficult to see, Daniel could make out wooden chairs scattered about. Some had been broken. Pictures that once hung on the walls were ripped apart. Pieces were scattered on the floor among the chairs. On the wall to the far left was a wide window that looked down onto the great assembly hall and the stage. A curtain hung on either side of the window. Near the corner of the farthest wall was a door with multiple locks. At the base of the door lay a large, mangy dog—asleep. In the center of the room was a strange pile of what looked like fur coats. They were rising and falling as though they were breathing. Daniel stepped farther into the room along the wall and to the left of Caleb toward the window. He walked around the others and instructed these warriors to circle the room as best they could. They spread out on either side of him.

"Why have you come here?" A gravelly, feminine voice

floated around the room, bouncing off the walls and ceiling and not revealing its source. The dog in the corner by the door lifted its head and moved closer to the corner as though it would pass through the wall if it could. Everyone stood like statues.

Caleb lifted his chin and spoke to the voice through the dust-filled air of the room. "You have taken what does not belong to you. We have come to send you back to the realm of Darkness from which you came and take back this base for the kingdom of Light."

Soft laughter bounced around the room. The female voice continued. "What makes you think you can send me anywhere? I was invited here. I was asked to come and destroy. You stand here with children." Then sternly the voice added, "I eat children for breakfast." The laughter returned even louder.

Caleb spoke more forcefully. "We have come to stop you in the name of the King. By his authority, you are evicted from this place."

A long tentacle came from under the pile of fur and lashed at the dog. "Tell them by whose authority I am here," the tentacle bellowed.

Lilly ran to the animal and wrapped her arms around its neck, deflecting the tentacle. A loud growl erupted from the fur, and the tentacle lifted to strike Lilly. Daniel ran toward Lilly, dropped to his knees, and slid on metal-covered shins. He exposed his breastplate to block the tentacle from striking Lilly. As the tentacle bounced off his breastplate and hit the ground, Daniel stood and brought his boot down on the long, rubbery protrusion. A loud squeal filled the room, and the tentacle withdrew into the mound of fur.

The room was quiet. Lilly hugged the dog more tightly and looked into its eyes. "Agh! This isn't a dog! It's a man!" Lilly let go of the animal and fell backward.

Laughter erupted again. "So you have found the one who allowed me to come here," the female voice sneered. Then she whispered, "Others allowed me to invite my companions to infiltrate the base."

Daniel turned and looked out the window that overlooked the Assembly Room. Michael ran over and looked too. "The people! They don't know what they have agreed to," said Daniel.

"Some know," added Michael.

Michael nudged Daniel. "Come with me. Perhaps this is a two-pronged attack." They paused next to Caleb, who looked at them and nodded.

"You are correct," said Caleb. "Go, and may our King go with you." Caleb smiled at them as they ran out the door. James and Mathew followed them. Then turning to Lilly, Caleb added, "Your love is your gift. Take this man out of here, and help him find the truth that he must rediscover."

With that, Lilly helped the man rise and leave the room.

It was at this point that those who remained noticed Mark had shrunk into the corner beside Caleb. Maria and John ran to his side. He had lost his armor and was huddled in the corner, shaking. Maria lifted her fallen friend and held him, whispering, "It's okay. Everything is okay. You lost your armor.

The Resonator Room

You need to put it back on. Do you remember the pieces?" Slowly they went back over the various pieces and what they meant, ending with the promises of the King.

Luke remained standing next to Caleb. Looking up, he asked, "So what is my gift?"

Caleb smiled and looked down at the five-foot-three-inch 16-year-old. "Luke, perhaps your gift is your courage to fight battles that would terrify others larger than you."

"Courage," Luke whispered. "I like that. I have had to learn to be brave in many situations. I do like that."

Suddenly, the fur covering flew up into the air. The creature revealed itself as a hideous blob etched with wrinkles, a disgusting mound of flesh, and tentacles that flailed in all directions like a deformed octopus. Each of the warriors circled the creature, preparing for the battle ahead. They stood stiff and steely-eyed with palms facing the creature and waited.

They all saw a small spark appear above the creature, and she screamed. The spark seemed to light the ceiling, growing larger until it created a broad opening. Luke pointed at it and exclaimed, "That's what happened when you showed up, Caleb." Streaks of white and blue light came through and touched the floor beside each of the warriors. The lights grew to form beautiful, tall figures with wings and full armor. Each carried a sword and a shield. With their shields, they protected the young warriors and aimed their swords at the creature in the middle of the room. To the right of Caleb, just past Luke, another arrival appeared in human form with blue, glowing armor encased with jewels. On his head sat a glittering, gold crown. "It is time," the kingly Knight answered.

"No!" screamed the blob on the floor.

"Yes, your authority has been revoked," responded the King calmly.

A faint voice was heard as though coming from a speaker. "I was lied to. I was afraid I was going to lose everything because we were unable to defeat the enemy. She promised me success and power and only gave me more fear. I don't know why I ever believed that witch. I am sorry. I return my allegiance to the King, the one source of truth—and love."

The pitiful creature screamed as the King's host grabbed it and took it up through the portal above them. The King then turned toward Caleb. "I see you have remembered what you learned many years ago. I hope you realize your commission has not ended. You have done very well." The King grabbed Caleb and hugged him. Releasing Caleb, the King placed his hands on Caleb's shoulders and smiled. The others looked on with surprise as the King gave each of them a hug and praised them. "Now I must go down and assist in the battle against the others." The King vanished, leaving Caleb and the King's new warriors in the room alone.

Rachel turned to face the window to see what was happening in the Assembly Room. "Look!" she said, pointing at the main stage. "The King is there!" Everyone ran to the window to watch.

CHAPTER 16

The Assembly Room

With the approval of Caleb, the four boys—Daniel, Michael, Matthew, and James—ran out of the room and hastily slid down the handrails. They made their way back to the door to the Resonator Room.

They burst through the door and smacked into an old woman, sending her to the floor sputtering and mumbling about ill-mannered children. The platters, paper plates, and paper coffee cups she had been carrying were now scattered around them on the floor. The boys tried to quickly help her pick up the objects and then ran through the main doors to the Assembly Room, apologizing all the way.

The old woman set the items on a nearby table and stepped to the stairwell to close the door. At that moment, Lilly and the filthy man knocked her down as they exited the stairway.

"Yuck! Why have you brought this creature down with you?

It's disgusting," the woman shrieked. She grabbed a broom and began beating the filthy man and Lilly, forcing them to the floor.

Lilly reached up and grabbed the broom from the woman. "You are disgusting," Lilly told the woman. "Can't you see? It is a poor soul, and we need to help him."

The woman looked closely at the man and drew in her breath. "It's the Commander. Where has he been all this time?"

"Trapped in the resonator," replied Lilly. "He was trapped by the creature of Darkness he invited here."

The old woman pulled a wet towel from her cleaning apron and began to wipe the Commander's face. "Why have you done this?" she asked. "Why have you betrayed the King?" Tears trickled down her cheeks, and her voice cracked.

The Commander tilted his head and looked into the eyes of the old woman. He answered softly, "We were losing ground. I was sure if I could make a truce with the enemy, we could get along and live in peace. I thought if we left her alone, she would leave us alone."

The woman responded softly in return. "We cannot negotiate with an enemy who hates us. We must drive out the Darkness. That has always been our mission."

"I know," said the Commander. "I was lied to. I was afraid I was going to lose everything because we were unable to defeat the enemy. She promised me success and power and only gave me more fear. I don't know why I ever believed that witch. I am sorry. I return my allegiance to the King, the one source of truth—and love."

Lilly hugged the man on the floor next to her. He smiled at Lilly and at the old woman.

The old woman smiled back at the Commander. "Then it is time. Young child, please help the Commander. There are water and clean towels on my cart. Do what you can." She smiled and looked toward the Assembly Room. "I now know why those young men came barreling through here. The battle is raging, and I have work to do." With that, she stood up, removed her apron, and touched a name plate on her chest. The name plate read "MINE and Lieutenant Zoe." The woman was suddenly enveloped in a full set of armor. Removing the sword from her belt, she lifted it high above her head and proclaimed, "Great and Mighty King, I stand with my free will to fight for you until your return. Fill me with your love and power to defeat the enemy and send it packing." A blue flame hit the tip of her sword like a lightning bolt, traveling down the sword and fully covering her.

The Commander sank back against the wall and smiled. "I had forgotten our command." He turned to the woman, calling her by name. "Lieutenant Zoe, I give you my command to defeat the enemy with all authority of the King." He then nodded to the woman who returned his nod and headed through the Assembly Room doors.

Daniel, Michael, and the others were inside shaking the people they could reach to wake them. They were telling them to use the key hanging about their necks to remove the chains that bound them, releasing their Free Will. As the people removed their chains, they stood in the aisles as though waiting for instructions. Deep in the assembly, a young girl stood up and began screaming that some were not following protocol. Many of those who had been energetic during the performance began to stand and shout. That caused many who were asleep to begin to wake from their slumber.

Lieutenant Zoe recognized the awakening spreading from the aisle and stopped to talk to Daniel, Michael, and the others. "You are doing the right thing. Keep it up." Then she pushed past them, heading for the front platform. Once on the stage, Lieutenant Zoe began to shout to the people who were waking up. "You have been lied to. Take back your Free Will. It has been stolen from you and locked with a key around your neck. Use it to unlock your chains. Stand up for the truth of the King. If you are still a child of the King, arise, and remove your chains. Push back the enemy and those who follow the call of Darkness. Our time has come." Zoe lifted her sword above her head and shouted, "In the name of the King!"

The people awakening from their drowsiness began unlocking their chains, rising from their seats, and moving to the aisles. Some, realizing they were free, left the room. Many began to raise their voices in defiance of Darkness or in honor of the King. Others began to move toward the front and climb onto the platform.

Lieutenant Commander Robertson stepped back toward the far end of the platform, spreading his arms as though to protect the young dancers who had been performing. The exotically dressed older woman and the young dancers were huddled together in the back corner of the platform. The King's warriors who had once been chained in the audience were arriving on the stage from steps on either side, passing others who were running off the stage. One of the dancers rushed an armor-clad individual who had reached the stage. She grabbed their sword and began swinging it wildly toward Lieutenant Commander Robertson. She screamed, "I will no longer be a part of this." Then she lunged at the Lieutenant Commander but missed him. He lost his balance and fell to the floor. One of the warriors picked up the dancer and carried her off the stage. Some came from behind the Lieutenant Commander and helped him to his feet.

The attendees split into two groups. The smaller, more boisterous crowd had been supporting the Lieutenant Commander. A few of them began to wave their arms and chant unintelligibly, while others threw fiery sticks at the large, awakening group.

Several of those who reawakened spread bluish, clear shields over the crowd, deflecting the fiery bolts that then fell harmlessly to the ground. Others, using their shields, pushed back the attackers.

The battle had not gone on long when Zoe seemed lost as to how to control the anarchy taking place before her. Then Daniel felt a shift as though a door had opened. A bright light fell onto the stage behind Lieutenant Zoe.

Lieutenant Zoe looked out over the Assembly Room and shouted, "Evil is defeated this day. Turn back to the way of the King, or leave this place. Our battle was never against our fellow creatures but against the Darkness. If your brother or sister will not renounce the evil, then he must leave in peace by order of the King."

Daniel turned to look at Zoe. She held her sword out in front of her toward the crowd. Behind her stood the King with his left hand on her right shoulder. He looked at Daniel and pressed the first finger of his right hand to his lips. Daniel nodded and looked back at Lieutenant Zoe. A soft, blue light emitted from the tip of her sword and grew, spreading out over the room like an atomic bomb. Everyone stopped what they were doing and turned to see the cause of the great light. Behind the King were three creatures, tall and clothed in white light and jewel-adorned armor with bright, bluish-white swords drawn.

Those with the shields seemed to gain strength and began pushing those in defiance through the doors and out of the building. Among those being removed were Lieutenant Commander Robertson and the exotically dressed older woman who had been on stage with him. One of the soldiers announced, "Anyone who will renounce Evil may return now. All others are banished." Once they were outside the base, the doors closed and locked behind them.

CHAPTER 17

Freedom

Daniel left the Assembly Room and stood in the Greeting Room. Looking around, he noticed that the lights in the hallway were brighter and the building seemed to be repairing itself.

The King, Lieutenant Zoe, and Michael met Daniel in the center of the Greeting Room. The Commander and Lilly joined them as Caleb and his group entered from the stairs. The door to the stairs was now gone. Many in both the Assembly Room and the Greeting Room were hugging and cheering after defeating the Darkness and running them out of the building. After things began to settle down, the main door opened, and people began filing in and asking about a King and a freedom they had heard of.

Daniel stood with the small group of the King's warriors in the center of the Greeting Room. All were facing the King. "Thank you," the King began. "You have completed this assignment. We have much to be grateful for." The King smiled at each of them. "Caleb," the King added, "I hope you are willing to return to duty for me when you go home." Caleb smiled and nodded to the King.

A portal opened behind the King, and Beth ran through to her father's side. Caleb smiled and picked up Beth. "I had fun, Daddy. Can we go home now? I'm getting tired." She laid her head on her father's shoulder.

"Yes, Little Bug, I think it's time to go home too." Caleb looked at the King who nodded. Then Caleb stepped through the portal Beth had just run through. The portal closed behind them.

Zoe looked at the King. "So does this mean you have returned?"

The King looked at Zoe and placed his hand on her shoulder. "No, Zoe, you have not completed your mission. You are to stand against the Darkness and bring more to the Light."

"But why don't you just wipe Darkness out for us?" Lilly asked the King.

The King patted Lilly's head and replied, "Because Darkness is already defeated. I have given you all the authority to continue your mission. You must learn to use that authority. Unfortunately, many choose not to believe that Darkness exists. If people continue to deny his existence, he can win by default."

John spoke up. "Yeah, it's easy to win a battle if your opponent isn't fighting you back."

"That's right, John," the King replied, smiling. "Remember,

the most important thing to do is stand for what you know is right. The book will teach you that."

Daniel turned to the King. "Samuel said my friends are in danger. I would very much like to check on them and see what I can do to help."

"Yes, Daniel," the King answered. "I will be going with you. Don't worry. We will not be too late." Turning to those who were staying, the King added, "Please continue to study your manual, and don't forget to reach out to me. I will miss you if you don't. And remember, I am always near." With that, the King hugged each of them and said, "I love you."

Finally, the King turned to the Commander and said, "It is time to bring the manual out of the closet and bring it back into the Assembly Room. Don't you agree?" The Commander nodded strongly. The King hugged him and said, "I love you." The Commander cried openly as Zoe handed him a clean rag from under her breastplate.

A new door appeared behind the King, and he moved toward it. The King turned and said, "Be strong and stand your ground. When I come again, it will not be a rescue mission but a victory celebration." Then the King and Daniel stepped through the door.

CHAPTER 18

Too Late

Daniel was right behind the King when they stepped through the door. A beautiful shoreline lapped a sandy beach to his right. To his left stretched a grassy knoll with several tents ready for rest. In front of him was a table covered with a feast. It would have been ideal except for the absence of his friends. Daniel collapsed to his knees, and tears filled his eyes. "I'm too late to help them."

"No! We are not!" the King exclaimed. "The Dragon would have you believe that we are, but you must have faith in my plans. Everything will work out for the best for everyone." The King reached down and lifted Daniel to his feet. "You must trust me. It will be all right. The trials are not to defeat you but to make you stronger." Then the King hugged Daniel tightly.

When the King released Daniel, he moved behind him and placed his hands on Daniel's shoulders. "Let me show you what really happened." Images like a 3D video formed around Daniel, and he watched his friends pass by him, chatting.

Someone recognized that Daniel was not there, and they all began guessing where he was. Alex was hoping he had made it home. Jessica quickly reassured them that the King knew what he was doing.

Once they noticed the table with the feast, they began to eat and taste the bounty of meats, vegetables, cakes, and cookies. Each of them ate to their full desire. Then, one by one, everyone went to the tents to relax and wait for Daniel and the King to arrive.

Karen was the last to remain at the table. She walked past the tents a distance away toward a forested area beyond them. She began calling into the forest. Four large, black, vulture-like birds circled the sky a few times and then landed about a foot from Karen. She pointed to the tents, and the birds swooped to them and began pecking at the children inside. The sleeping kids appeared from the tents and began complaining about the ground, the tents, the food, and even the fact that Daniel was not there.

The four blackbirds continued to walk among the children, unseen, pecking and biting them. At first, Jessica was trying to calm the others down until she suddenly began yelling at the others as well. A black mist settled over the camp, and one by one they fell to the ground, asleep. After they fell, the blackbirds picked them up and took them away. The birds continued to return and scoop up more kids until they had taken all of them. Finally, the birds picked up and took Karen away as well.

Daniel closed his eyes and breathed a sigh. When he opened

them, the vision was gone and so were his friends. "What are those blackbirds?" Daniel asked softly.

A beautiful woman with long, blonde hair and a white, lustrous, flowing gown stepped out from the tent that was closest to Daniel. "Those blackbirds are creatures of evil waiting for anyone who has given up and is ready to let go of the light of Love," she said. "They peck at their victims to demoralize them and finally drag them to their nest near the Dragon's Den. There, they tear the flesh from their victims' bodies and drag them deep into the den. They are creatures of destruction and death." As she spoke, her voice became softer. "These they did not take to their nest but directly to the dungeons of the Dragon."

The King pointed to the beautiful creature. "Daniel, this is Sophia. She will aid us."

Daniel looked at Sophia and then turned back toward the King. "Where is Gabriella? I didn't see her after the battle."

The King responded to Daniel's concern. "Her mission is ended. She has returned to her little house with Samuel. We may see her again, but know that she is all right."

Daniel looked toward the trees in the distance for a long time and then asked, "Are they still here? Can they get us?"

Sophia responded. "Like vultures, they are only interested in those things that don't or can't fight back. We are safe from them. But there are other creatures who follow the Dragon, and they are much worse. We will need to prepare to meet them." Sophia motioned for Daniel to follow her and said, "For now, it is time to rest and recharge."

Fresh food appeared on the table as if from nowhere. It was laden with Daniel's favorites and some he was not familiar with. Sophia gracefully moved to the table and set some beautiful greens on a white, pristine plate. Daniel paused on his way to the table, not seeing anything that resembled his favorite Ranch or Thousand Island dressing. He added, "Oh, I don't eat salad without salad dressing."

Sophia responded with a very proper smile. "Don't worry. You don't have to eat anything you don't want to. But you should at least try the salad. It is packed with nutrients, and you might find you don't want salad dressing." Sophia sat on a chair that had not been there a moment before.

Daniel replied, "Okay." He came to the table to more closely inspect the strange leaves. He picked up a single leaf and turned it over. One side was a deep purplish-green while the other side was light gray with red veins running through it. It appeared quite fresh with a slight smell of mint. He placed the leaf on the tip of his tongue where it melted, leaving a slight buttery taste. He put the rest of the leaf into his mouth and felt the sensation fill his whole mouth, leaving a sweet tingle. "This is awesome!" he exclaimed.

Sophia smiled. "Keep eating, and that feeling will spread. Try another one. They all taste fantastic, and each has a purpose for healing and restoration. You will need your strength as you continue your training."

Daniel sat and began to try the new flavors along with his own familiar foods. After a few minutes of a bite of this and a bite of that, he realized he was tired. "Is the food supposed to make you sleepy?" Daniel abruptly stood up and asked, "Is this a trap?" Daniel was beginning to wonder if he had been stupid. He had never been drugged before and wondered if this was what it felt like. He could not fight the fatigue.

Sophia responded, "No, you are exhausted. Look! There is a tent with a pallet inside. You need to rest. We will protect you." Standing behind a small tent that was not previously there were two creatures resembling Dominion. Daniel found a pallet inside the tent just as Sophia had said. Since the alternative meant falling asleep standing up, he aimed for the pile of pillows and blankets and let go of the dream.

Daniel had hoped he would be in his own bed at home when he woke up, but that didn't happen. He slowly got up from the blankets and pillows and exited the tent, hoping his friends were at the table enjoying another banquet. They were not. The worst part of all was knowing he was the one who brought Karen into their group. He had believed her when she said she wanted to follow the King. He was the one who brought the danger into the camp. It was his fault.

"Daniel," Sophia called. "It's time to finish your training. There is much ahead of you."

Daniel staggered out of his tent. "Tell me, is it possible to get my friends back?"

Sophia looked Daniel up and down. "Do you know what it means to stand?"

Daniel looked at Sophia curiously. "Yes, I'm doing that right now. I am standing,"

The corner of Sophia's mouth raised slightly as she shook

her head. "No. You are standing, but not in the confidence of the King. Tell me, Daniel, who are you?"

Daniel shook his head, not understanding the question. "I'm Daniel Pierce of Ear . . ."

"No!" Sophia shouted. "You are Daniel Pierce, son of the Almighty. Earth is where you live, not where you belong. You must always remember that or you will fall under the spell of the Darkness. You will believe all is lost and that Darkness has won. That is his only weapon. You need your shield to block his tempting arrows. Where is your armor?"

Daniel stared at Sophia for a moment and then shrugged. Sophia continued. "We put our armor on and take it off through the decisions we make every day. *Faith* is your shield. Where is the stick you found in the trunk?"

Daniel reached into his pocket, wondering if it was still there. He pulled out the object. It was almost five inches long and about the diameter of his thumb. The surface had the markings of a small tree limb but was made from some type of bluish metal. The word *Faith* was engraved on the side in gold. Daniel asked, "How is this supposed to help me?" He held it out in front of him, twisting his wrist as though he had a mighty sword. Suddenly, Daniel noticed a knight standing silently a few feet away yet seemingly unaware of Daniel's movements or questions. Daniel said, "So really, what do I do with this? Does it turn into a sword like a lightsaber?" The knight remained stoic while Sophia watched silently. Daniel stabbed forward with the stick and then swung his arm in a great circle and yelled, "Abracadabra!" Still nothing happened, except Sophia fell off the chair she was sitting on. When Daniel looked at her, she was laughing hysterically. She quickly regained her composure and sat back on the chair, straightening her dress.

When Daniel looked up at the knight again, he noticed that the knight was standing with one arm held up, parallel with the ground, bent at the elbow, and his wrist turned inward as though he were holding a shield in front of him. Daniel extended his arm and bent his elbow, holding the metal stick straight, pointing up and down. Remembering the phrase used for the helmet, he said, "Great King, give me the power and authority to defend your people."

Without warning, there was a soft whoosh of wind. The helmet, belt, and shoes reappeared as before. The stick extended in length and wrapped itself around Daniel's forearm every three inches. Daniel released his grip on the stick, which now stopped just before his elbow. He was unsure if he could move his hand or his arm but was surprised to find the metal quite pliable. He tried to unwind the device from his arm, but it wouldn't budge. Although it was on his arm, it didn't hinder his movements.

Daniel felt something in the palm of his hand. Looking in his hand, he noticed that the device was glowing with a brilliant white light. The light grew straight up and straight down and then spread across to either side. Through its clear glow, Daniel saw the Knight lift a crossbow and fire. For a moment, Daniel panicked until the arrow hit the force field the device had created and abruptly fell to the ground.

Sophia walked across the opening toward Daniel and patted

him on the shoulder. "Do you remember the arrows thrown by the Darkness in the Assembly Room battle?" she asked.

Daniel nodded, and Sophia continued. "Those arrows become thoughts implanted in the mind. Just because a thought crosses your mind doesn't make it your thought unless you agree with it. An example of this is the thoughts of guilt you had when you woke up just now. Your friends are not in danger because of you, but the Dragon wants you to think they are. He knows if you ever push past the insecurity, doubt, or fear within you, if you choose instead to believe the truth of Love and live in accordance with it, you'll erect a shield of protection that will smother his plans. Your shield will cause his fiery arrows to fizzle. The Dragon likes using a misleading, repetitive pattern, hoping you'll never catch onto it. He wants you to panic and not wait on the King. Always remember, the King is our protector and shield. It is his faith and our reliance on his truths that guard us. Our faith is the process of walking in the truth of the King and his love. It means living that belief." Sophia held her arm up like she was carrying a shield and stepped forward as though pushing through something. "Our shield allows us to advance despite adverse circumstances. It gives clear vision and protection."

Sophia stepped back and lowered her arms. Daniel turned to look at the Knight, but he was gone. Sophia continued. "The key here is action or inaction. It is a test that shows us what we believe to be true. You must adapt your behavior, your decisions, and ultimately your whole lifestyle so they align with what the King has asked of you—without needing to see evidence that it will all work out in the end. When you can't see what the outcome will be, an act of faith becomes a shield of protection to guard against the enemy's attacks."

"Okay," Daniel said as he stood up straight. "So how does this help me free my friends? How do I rescue them?" Daniel heard the now familiar sound of a portal opening behind him and turned to see the King. *Was he not here the whole time?* Daniel thought.

"Daniel," the King began. "Your friends were taken to the dungeons of the Dragon. You will have to face the Dragon in order to bargain for their freedom. This portal will take you to his fortress. Remember, I am always with you." Then the King faded from sight.

It's amazing how he can move between dimensions like that, Daniel pondered.

Sophia turned Daniel to face the portal. "What is your choice? Are you going after your friends or not?" Daniel didn't even turn to face Sophia or respond to her question but ran through the open portal.

CHAPTER 19

Sacrifice

Daniel stepped into a large, oblong room that stretched out before him with walls covered in riveted metal. Scattered about the room were couches, and seated on the couches were military-dressed people chatting with each other. Some were smoking strange pipes, and their thin smoke hovered around their heads. *I'm so tired of getting dumped out in a dark room of people, not knowing if they are for me or against me,* Daniel thought. He let out a sigh and mused, *I'm also tired of ending up by myself somewhere.*

Daniel frowned as he began inspecting his new location. Sophia had told him this was the primary domain of the Dragon. It was dark, arid, warm, and lacking comfort. However, the various creatures there didn't seem to mind; they didn't care about much of anything, not even Daniel's presence.

To either side were smaller rooms that opened to the main hall. Several of the walls of the main room as well as the side rooms displayed what appeared to be fine silks and tapestries.

Some walls had paintings of images with no shape or form, created in dingy shades of gray. The rooms were filled with what Daniel would consider expensive furnishings. Looking closer, he noticed thread-bare or torn fabrics, and the furniture was nicked and broken.

A doorway on the far wall opened, and a short, dirty man dressed in what appeared to be Roman attire entered the main hall pushing a small utility cart through the door. He had on a long shirt that hung to his knees, and there was a piece of fabric draped across his chest and pinned to the material on each of his shoulders. He looked to be about three feet tall and had stubby legs and short arms. His bald head seemed unusually large for his size. As he pushed the cart into a side room and then the other, the people scoffed at him and spoke rudely, complaining about bad service. They at once went back to lounging and doing what appeared to be nothing of importance. The little man appeared not to notice Daniel. So when the man went back through the door, Daniel followed him.

Beyond the door, the walls were no longer clad in metal but were rough-hewn rock that formed a tunnel. The adjoining rooms on either side of the corridor were no more than large alcoves. The walls were bare with the rock face showing. The furnishings were sparse and visibly worn. There were several people occupying them. A few of the rooms had pallets with torn blankets where people were resting, but there were no actual beds.

Daniel continued to follow the little man down the long corridor. The people they passed didn't seem to notice him.

They appeared oblivious to their surroundings, conversing with unseen others or muttering obscenities to themselves. Occasionally, someone would look up and scream at him, but if he kept moving, they left him alone.

As he walked through the labyrinth, it sometimes sloped downward but just as quickly angled back up. It turned and twisted, branching off in random directions, making it nearly impossible to find his way back. At one point, the alcoves ceased, and there were no doorways to allow entry or exit. There was only a long hallway.

Daniel's steps slowed down, and he wondered if he had made the right decision to face such a powerful adversary. *What made me think I could do anything to help my friends?* he asked himself. He remembered the name badge and touched it lightly. He felt the breastplate on his chest and strong shoes on his feet. His helmet covered his head. Daniel stopped and smiled to himself, remembering the King was somehow with him.

Daniel heard a voice. "Remember, if the creatures approach you, they must obey you and leave you alone because you carry my authority. Make your way carefully, and know that I love you." Daniel stopped completely, closed his eyes, and thanked the King.

When he opened his eyes, the little man was directly in front of him, looking up. "Did you really think I didn't see you following me?" the man smirked. Daniel took a quick, deep breath.

"I know why you are here," the little man continued. "They

always want me to take them to the Supreme One. What will you trade me to see him? I have the largest collection of anyone here. I know how to get what I want. What do you have that I might want?" He continued to poke at Daniel who tried to think of something he had that he could offer the little man.

Then the voice came again. "Look in your pocket."

What do I have in my pocket? I'm not going to give this little man my shield, Daniel thought to himself.

"Just look in your pocket. Trust me," the voice pushed him. Daniel reached into his pocket and found a small lump of what looked like gold. The voice laughed and replied, "No, just iron pyrite. Trust me."

"What is that?" smirked the little man. "What have you got there for me?" He tried desperately to see what Daniel was holding.

Slowly, Daniel held out his hand to show the little man what he was holding. The man grabbed the small stone, examined it, and said, "What is this? It looks very special—very special indeed." Looking up at Daniel, he said, "I'll take it. I'm sure it's nothing of importance." The little man paused. "It's pretty enough. I'll take you to the Supreme One." The little man winked at Daniel. "And I won't even tell him you're coming." A smile stretched across his face as he spun around and headed down the corridor. Then he stopped and turned toward Daniel. "Of course, I can't say no one else has warned him." And the smile grew even larger. Waving his short arm, he said, "Come on. We must hurry."

Soon they came to a small pair of doors. The little man

pushed a button on the wall, and the doors slid open. He gestured for Daniel to enter. Daniel paused a moment and then stepped past the little man and entered what appeared to be an elevator. The little man pushed the last button on the bottom and stepped back into the hall. "Good luck. Don't blame me when you come back as toast." Then the little man turned and bent over, laughing. "Toast!"

The doors closed, leaving Daniel alone. He waited to feel the elevator's descent, but he never felt anything. It took a while for the doors to open again. Daniel half expected to be back in the hallway or find that he had passed through another portal. He wondered if maybe he had. When the doors opened, he stepped into a small room with rough stone walls that held only a wooden torch in a metal mounting. Daniel removed the torch and placed his hand gently on top, imagining the torch was lit. The torch emitted a soft, blue light. When Daniel turned to replace the torch, he noticed the walls were charred. He spoke out loud to no one, "I have the authority of the King before a defeated foe."

Daniel then turned to face an expansive cave with various large stalagmites and stalactites randomly scattered throughout. A soft glow emitted from the floor of the chamber. Further inspection revealed that it was covered with tall piles of gemstones of all shapes and colors, each about the size of the palm of his hand. They seemed to glow from within.

Daniel reached down and picked up one of the gems near his feet. A woman's face that he didn't recognize appeared on the largest facet of the jewel. She looked tired and unhappy.

He replaced the stone and picked up two more. The face on one was that of a man. He appeared angry. On the other, the face was distorted so Daniel couldn't tell if it was a man or a woman. This face also appeared unhappy. Daniel put these gemstones back on the floor of the cave.

As he was rising, he heard the snort of what sounded like a large animal of some kind. Smoke filled the atmosphere in the cave, and on a far wall Daniel could just make out the shape of a large dragon resting on top of a very tall pile of jewels.

"I have been waiting for you, boy. You are very important to me. I have been watching you and your little friends. Did you know that? At each of your moments of testing, I have been there overhead." The Dragon spoke slowly and softly with a low pitch as though he wanted Daniel to understand with great clarity what he was saying. Daniel stood very still, waiting to hear what the Dragon had to say—waiting for the moment when the Dragon would show himself and his lies would be clear.

Slowly, the Dragon's smoky exhalation wrapped itself around one of the cave's pillars and floated toward Daniel. The Dragon followed his smoke trail and turned to face its new guest. The smoke dissipated, and the Dragon's scales shone in the dim light. They almost appeared as if they had some type of eerie light source within. However, it didn't take long for Daniel to realize that it was only a reflection of the light coming from the gemstones. The gemstones seemed to be giving the Dragon his sense of power. Daniel wondered if the people were the source of the Dragon's power. That would explain a lot.

Sacrifice

Daniel moved carefully along the cave wall, avoiding stepping on any of the gemstones. When he stood as close to the Dragon as possible, he stopped and said, "I have come for my friends. You have taken them without their permission and without cause."

The Dragon laughed. "That is not entirely true." He moved a little closer to Daniel. "I heard you exclaim that you didn't want them. You wished they were not your problem. You even wished you had never been born." The Dragon snorted. "I could have taken you as well if you had been there and not driven my soldiers from your little allied base. Don't you worry. I will regain my ground there. They will stop attending to the battle, and I will be back. There are always those who are not watchful, who don't believe I exist." The Dragon laughed.

For a moment, the Dragon paused and thought. "You know, those are the easiest to manipulate. They do not protect themselves from an enemy they do not believe exists." The Dragon laughed even harder this time.

"I take it back," Daniel screamed. Placing his hands on either side of his head, he yelled, "I take it back. That's not what I meant. I demand their release." The Dragon laughed even harder.

Then the Dragon stopped and looked at Daniel for a moment and seemed to change the subject. "I noticed you are wearing your armor. How militant of you!" The Dragon paused again. "So you have been listening to the King. But of course, he is not here with you, is he?"

Daniel stood even straighter. "He is here. He is always with me."

The Dragon harrumphed. "I see. He told you that. But I bet he didn't tell you before sending you on this great adventure that you cannot just traipse in here and make demands of me. I also have rights, and I demand my rights."

The Dragon circled another column, moving closer to Daniel. "I have what is mine, and I only accept trades for what is mine." He stopped his approach, sat back on his hind legs, and put his pointing finger to his mouth. He tapped it a few times on an exposed tooth and questioned Daniel. "I'll tell you what." He leaned forward on all four limbs. "I will trade all your friends if you reject the King and agree to side with me. What are they worth to you? Tell me."

Daniel stiffened and turned to face the cave wall. He stretched out his arms to either side and saw his shadow form a cross on the wall. "I will not reject the King, but I will trade my life for my friends."

Daniel saw his shadow begin to grow larger. Suddenly, the Dragon lifted his tail, and Daniel watched the barbed tip of it head for his shadow. "I knew you would come," the Dragon hissed at the King who was standing behind him. "I knew this would bring you here. I knew you would do anything for him. Now you will see what defeat feels like. Now I have you, and I have won!" Daniel braced for the impact and imagined the pain of the spike piercing his chest. The Dragon screamed. Daniel felt nothing. Nothing touched him.

Daniel turned around to see the King holding the Dragon

down on the pile of gemstones closest to Daniel. The King released his hold on the Dragon who then slithered back down into the cave. "I have rights. I will see you in court," the Dragon shouted. "You will not get them back without a proper trade!" He continued to scream as he retreated. "I told you, boy, that I would get what I wanted." The Dragon kept yelling from the distant corridors of the cavern, his voice echoing off the walls.

The King turned to Daniel and patted his shoulder. "Don't worry about the Dragon. He has no real power over you. Just look at him. He keeps thinking he can beat me. I keep showing him who has won this battle. I made a show of him before, but he still tries to defeat me. He can't. He can only win when he is allowed to—when you let him."

Daniel looked back at the Dragon's retreat. His scales had no beauty to them. The light of the gemstones that had been reflecting off his scales had made him appear more powerful than he was. *It has been a gigantic lie all along*, Daniel thought.

With that, Daniel turned to face the King. "That was your shadow I saw on the wall taking my place. I don't understand," Daniel replied.

The King smiled at Daniel. "What does your breastplate say?"

Daniel gingerly felt the breastplate where the badge had been. "It says *MINE*."

The King responded, "And what does that mean to you?"

Daniel thought for a moment. "I belong to you?"

"Exactly," exclaimed the King.

Daniel gently shook his head and then thought to himself, *I belong?*

"Wait!" he addressed the King. "What do you mean by 'I belong to you'? I thought I was now free." Daniel scowled. He didn't like the idea of belonging to anyone. People had always said he belonged to them, and that never worked out well.

"Belonging to me is not like that," the King explained. "Do you remember when a neighbor tried to hurt Angel, your little puppy? You put yourself between the neighbor and Angel to protect him. You always took care of Angel. He belonged to you, and you loved him with all your heart. I claim ownership of you in order to bring you under my protection and into my love."

Daniel thought about his Malamute puppy, remembering Angel as more than just a pet. He was Daniel's best friend. He followed him everywhere and took care of Daniel as much as Daniel took care of him. He talked to Angel like he was a person. When they were apart, Daniel was sad. Angel was the epitome of love and joy.

A chuckle rose from within the King. "I don't think of you as a pet, though. I just love you that much." Daniel sat smiling. It felt good to belong.

Suddenly, a door appeared on the wall of the cave. "Daniel," the King spoke gravely. "My kingdom is subject to laws set from the beginning of time. We will have to go and petition for your friends' release."

"But if you knew I couldn't get my friends from the Dragon, why did you send me here?" Daniel asked.

"Because I needed you to see who the Dragon was and to show you that he has no power over you," the King replied.

Daniel nodded his head in response. Daniel and the King walked through the portal.

CHAPTER 20

Judgment

Daniel stepped out of the doorway into a huge, marble hallway. It was lined with tall, white, marble columns. The doors along the hallway were white, and when Daniel touched one, it looked and felt like it had been formed from a giant pearl. The doorframes were inlaid with gold images of leaves and flowers. The tile on the floor had intricate shapes of various colors of marble imbedded in it as though they had formed there naturally. The veins in the marble were like gemstones of every color. The mix of texture and color might have seemed chaotic but was miraculously beautiful. Creatures of every kind walked past Daniel. Several turned and stared. Some even bowed to him. Then Daniel realized that the King was standing to one side just behind him.

Daniel turned, smiled at the King, and for the first time noticed that the King was a few inches shorter than he was. "I'm so glad you came through with me this time," Daniel said sheepishly. "I wasn't sure how I was going to plead my case or my friends' cases."

The King placed his hand beneath Daniel's chin and smiled. "You will plead guilty, of course. The truth is that you *are* guilty, are you not?" The King's voice was so sweet and loving that all Daniel could do was nod as he looked into eyes of deep pools. In those eyes, he felt a love he had never known before. He never wanted to look away.

Slowly Daniel turned, and the King placed one arm around his shoulder. Daniel wondered if he had shrunk or if the King had suddenly grown tall enough to do so. Together they walked down the hall to the main courtroom through two huge pearly doors that looked as though they never closed.

The courtroom inside was so massive that Daniel could barely see the other side. In the distance was a high throne covered in a thick white cloud. To the left of the throne was a smaller, empty throne. Just in front of that was a large delegation of white-clothed creatures talking among themselves. They appeared especially important to the proceedings. Daniel wondered if they were a jury or something similar. To the right and near the front was a small enclosure of short, wooden rails. It looked like it could only hold about four people. Daniel guessed that if a creature was large, it couldn't hold more than one or two. For now, it was empty. Daniel was wondering if that was his destination.

The rest of the courtroom consisted of rows of marble benches with ornately decorated legs. The courtroom was full of people, and the King led Daniel to a seat at the end of a bench near the front. At the King's request, those on the bench scooted down to allow Daniel room. The King remained standing beside Daniel.

Creatures continued to fill the courtroom until what appeared to be the primary creature of the jury stood and proclaimed, "The court is now in session, presided by Our Most Honorable Judge." He sat back down and waited, as did all the people in the courtroom.

Daniel held his breath, waiting to see Our Most Honorable Judge. Suddenly, the King stepped forward to a podium in front of the throne, an equal distance from the jury, the wooden enclosure, and the cloud-covered throne. "Excuse me. If it pleases Our Most Honorable Judge, I request to speak first on behalf of one who is very special to me. He is requesting a trade with his accuser for the lives of his friends. They also are special to me."

The King stood in silence, waiting for a reply. The entire courtroom was also silent. Daniel wasn't sure if this was proper protocol, but he wanted to believe that the King knew what he was doing. He had to believe that. It was his only choice.

A voice came from every direction like layers upon layers. "How can I refuse a special request from you?" A sincere feeling of love intensified within Daniel until he wasn't sure he could hold it in any longer. He slowly sneaked his hand up to wipe a tear from his cheek. *Where did that come from?* When Daniel looked up, the King once again stood next to him and motioned for him to rise and walk to the podium. Daniel complied.

Judgment

The Primary of the Council, as was explained to Daniel, stood up and began to question him. "Name, please."

Daniel remembered what Sophia had told him on the seashore. "Daniel Pierce of Earth, Child of the One True King." Daniel stood at the podium as tall as he could and stated his name.

The Primary asked, "What are your crimes?" Then looking up angrily, he added, "Where is your accuser?"

Everyone was looking around the courtroom when the Dragon appeared from one side and walked on his hind legs toward the wooden enclosure. As he walked forward, he morphed from a dragon to a human-like creature. He stood tall and dark with a flowing cape of dragon scales reflecting the light in the room. "I know. I know. I'm late." He dramatically swung his arms toward the cloud on the throne. "I wouldn't be late if you wouldn't make it so hard for me to get here." The Dragon made another dramatic gesture and added, "One little mistake and you banish me from your . . ."

The King cleared his throat, and the Dragon fell silent. The King looked at the Primary who now directed his questions to the Dragon. "What are the crimes you have against this boy and his colleagues?"

"Well, I'll tell you," the Dragon squeaked and cleared his throat. "This young boy was under my authority." The King coughed, and the Dragon cleared his throat. "As I was saying, this young boy asked for his friends to no longer be his problem. He invited an enemy of this King into the camp and then left, giving me great opportunity. So I removed them.

As I was removing them, they began fighting in a very hateful manner, asking for evil to befall the others. We all know that the thoughts of the heart equate the action. And finally, no one has regretted their actions."

Daniel looked at the King. "Is that really all he is complaining about? Those seem like petty charges. How can something so small be so big in your kingdom?"

The King responded in a quiet tone. "Daniel, it is important to understand that thoughts are powerful here. The only thing more powerful than our thoughts is our words. Words spoken by one of authority are creative. They can create reality. That is why the Book admonishes us to bring every thought into captivity."

Daniel looked down at his feet. "Then what can I do?" he asked, looking back at the King.

"Plead guilty, and ask to separate yourself from your actions words, thoughts, and anything that negatively affects others. Ask that they become null and void." The King then turned to face the court while still talking softly to Daniel. "I will do the rest."

The Primary turned to face Daniel and said, "How do you plead?"

Daniel turned to face the court and answered loudly, "I plead guilty to all the charges and ask to be separated from all words, thoughts, and actions that have affected me and others."

The man-dragon laughed. "Yes!" Turning to the cloud, he exclaimed, "He has admitted his guilt. You must sentence him and his friends to death and my care." The man-dragon then turned to Daniel and smiled a smile that only a dragon could make.

Daniel drew in his breath and whispered to the King, "What's the rest?"

The King solemnly walked to a basin not far from the witness stand. He turned toward Daniel and said, "Daniel, do you freely accept the offer of my will over yours?"

Daniel stared at the King and answered, "Yes, I do." Daniel stood silent.

"Do you understand that in doing so, you become my property, my beloved?" asked the King.

Daniel furrowed his forehead but continued to stare at the King. "Yes, I do," Daniel answered.

The King went on as he stood next to the basin. "Do you understand that the transgression you have admitted to requires a payment of death?" The King looked at Daniel and smiled as he nodded.

Daniel's heart began to beat rapidly. *What is happening? I trust the King. I trust the King. I trust the King.* Daniel looked at the King and answered a little more quietly. "Yes, I understand that and beg the court's forgiveness."

The King dipped his cupped hand into the red liquid that filled the basin. He spoke as he walked over to Daniel. "Since I have already paid the price for the forgiveness of all sins, I trade my life for Daniel's and his friends' lives." The King leaned over to Daniel and whispered, "Ask that your case be covered by my blood that I shed to cover your sins."

Daniel shouted, "I accept the trade of my life for the King's and ask that my case and those of my friends be covered by his blood as payment for our sins and transgressions."

The King sprinkled the red liquid over Daniel, leaning in close to his ear and saying, "You learn fast, my child." When Daniel looked up at the King, he once again felt the warmth of incredible love envelop him.

Neither of them noticed nor could they hear the screams of the Dragon over the cheers of the others in the courtroom. "They still belong to me!" the Dragon shrieked. "If they have rejected you, they belong to me." With that, the Dragon stepped out of his wooden stand and turned to leave. As he did, his human shape changed back to a dragon lost in darkness.

What Daniel did notice was a giant, kind, human-like face surrounded by a mane of white, curly hair as it leaned down from the cloud on the throne. Again, the voice came from every direction like layers upon layers. "I am pleased with my son." Looking directly at Daniel, he added, "I am quite pleased with you, Daniel."

"Thank you, Sir," Daniel replied, smiling up at his face. Then the face dissipated.

Daniel and the King hugged. Daniel asked, "Why did you do this?"

The King replied, "Because you are that important to me. I love you that much. All of you are important to me. I love you all. Now take the gemstones of your friends and family." The King handed Daniel a pouch with several crystals like the ones in the Dragon's cave. "We have saved them; however, even though you have their gemstones, each one must choose their own path. Go now, and everything will be all right. Don't worry about the Dragon. He has no real power over you. Remember what you saw in the cave. Trust in me, and go."

Daniel grabbed his bag of gems and raced to the hallway and the door where he had entered. He no longer feared the Dragon or his followers. Even if he didn't feel the King's presence, Daniel would not fear. The King had promised he would take care of Daniel and his friends, and Daniel believed him—some way, somehow.

CHAPTER 21

Rescue

Daniel stepped through the doorway expecting to return to the Dragon's cave, but he didn't. Instead, he stepped into a metal-clad, riveted hallway. It wasn't like the earlier one. The lighting was brighter, and it was cold there. It also didn't show signs of time. But it didn't look new either.

There was no one in the corridor this time, and Daniel let out a sigh of relief as he checked his surroundings. The hallway stretched in either direction for what appeared to be forever.

Daniel was contemplating which direction he should go when the door behind him opened. He jumped to the other side of the corridor with his back against the wall and placed his hand in his pocket, searching for his shield. The light beyond the door was so bright that Daniel had to place his other arm in front of his face to block as much of the light as he could. The door shut, and Daniel brought his arm down. There stood Gabriella.

Rescue

Daniel ran to little Gabriella, dropped to his knees, and hugged her tightly. So much had happened since their encounter on the allied base. Gabriella held him tightly. "Do not worry. It was not your fault," she said. "That is just what the evil one wants you to think." She wiped a tear from his cheek. "Have faith, and trust in the King. He knows what he is doing. Now we must go find your friends."

Daniel looked at Gabriella's smiling face. Leaning back on his heels, he asked, "But where do we start?"

Gabriella pulled out the device she had used in the ice planet and aimed it in each direction down the corridor. Turning to Daniel, she asked, "May I see the gemstones the King gave you?"

"You know about these?" Daniel asked as he pulled a leather pouch from his pocket and removed the stones for Gabriella to see.

"Of course," Gabriella replied. She aimed the device at the gems and then in each direction down the hallway. The device had been glowing a dim blue light, but during her final sweep, it began to suddenly become very bright. "This way to your friends."

Daniel grabbed her arm and said, "How does that thing know where they are?"

Gabriella smiled. "The Spirit always knows." She then headed in the direction the light had shone. As they traveled, Daniel told Gabriella about his adventures with the bird-like creatures and the courtroom. Gabriella smiled and nodded with each story. When Daniel finished, she stopped him and said, "I know. Samuel and I were watching. We saw the whole thing. You were a true warrior of the King. Now we must rescue your friends."

Daniel looked at Gabriella for a moment and shook his head. Turning back revealed a door Daniel had not noticed before. Gabriella motioned to the door, and Daniel placed his hand on it and stated, "By the authority of the King, I release this door and command it to open for us." He heard a faint click, and the door opened silently. Daniel pushed on the door and entered a dark, medieval dungeon of rough brick covered in filth and grime. The walls were lined with cells closed by iron gates, but he couldn't see who was in any of the cells. Instead, he could read markings above each cell with words such as DEPRESSION, UNFORGIVENESS, HATE, SELF-LOATHING, LIAR, THIEF, MURDERER, and REBELLION.

"I told you they are not very imaginative," scoffed Gabriella as she followed Daniel into the dungeon.

"Where are the guards?" Daniel asked.

"Did I not tell you they are arrogant and self-assured?" questioned Gabriella. She moved to the center of the room and placed her orb on the floor. After instructing Daniel to place the gemstones around the orb, she spoke. "Oh, Most Precious King, give us the power to see the truth." The light of the gemstones glowed brighter, but the light of the orb remained soft. Daniel quietly whispered to the orb, "Most Precious King, please show us your power." Suddenly, the light from the orb grew until it exploded, filling the room and the cells encircling the walls. Daniel felt himself blown backward from the orb and wondered if that was what a bomb explosion felt like. Looking around, he saw shattered light fixtures on the walls. Light came from every direction as bright as a thousand suns, yet his eyes didn't seem to react to it. Looking around the room, he noticed that the cell doors seemed to have been blown inward, and each of his friends slowly appeared from their cells.

Gabriella picked up a bright, purple stone and stood in front of Jessica. Offering the stone to Jessica in cupped hands, she asked, "Jessica do you repent of the act of unforgiveness toward others?" Daniel noticed the engraving above her door and looked back at Jessica. When her eyes met Daniel's, she lowered her gaze.

Looking back at Gabriella, she replied, "Yes, I do." And she took the stone Gabriella offered her.

Next, Gabriela picked up another stone with a beautiful pink hue and stood before Samantha. The engraving above Samantha's door read SELF-LOATHING. As Jessica's eyes looked up at Samantha's door, Samantha appeared to be trying not to cry. Gabriella held Samantha's stone up to her and asked, "Samantha, do you know how much the King loves you, and how much he wants you to love yourself as much as he loves you?" Samantha turned to look at Jessica who smiled and nodded in agreement.

Samantha smiled and replied, "Yes, I do." Gabriella offered the pink stone to Samantha who accepted the stone from her.

Next, Gabriella took a stone to Justin's cell that read HATRED. Justin looked around the room at each of his companions. He had tried to stay quiet throughout the adventure, but he could no longer do so. Gabriella offered a deep, royal blue stone to Justin and asked, "Justin, it is time for you to choose your future. Do you want to continue to harbor hate for your fellow man, or do you want to accept the love of the King for yourself and extend that love to others?"

Justin looked at the others, expecting rejection from them. Surprisingly, the looks he received were only kind. Justin finally turned to look at Daniel whose hand was extended, offering a handshake of friendship. Justin's expression softened as he looked at Daniel's extended hand. Smiling, he stepped forward to accept it. "I think I will. Yes, I do indeed believe I will." Then Justin smiled at Daniel, and each of them stepped back to watch Gabriella complete her ritual with the others.

Gabriella took the rest of the stones from the pile and repeated the affirmation with each person in the group. Finally, she came to Karen who looked at the others and declined her stone, retreating into her now unlocked cell.

"That is your choice," Gabriella said as she laid the stone on the floor in front of Karen's cell and turned back to Daniel. "That is everyone." She turned and picked up her orb and moved toward the door they had entered. "The enemy will come to see what the explosion was. It is time to leave."

Daniel and the others gave one last look at Karen's cell. Daniel looked up at the engraving that read REBELLION. Then Daniel and the others went out the door behind Gabriella and back into the bleak hallway.

Gabriella lifted her orb, and the light pointed back the way they had come. About halfway down the hall, they entered a stairwell and began climbing a winding staircase toward the surface. Daniel, who was directly behind Gabriella, asked, "How far away is the door?"

Gabriella whispered back to him and the others. "The portal is on the other side of their base."

Jessica looked up the stairwell and asked, "Couldn't they have copied an elevator?" Others agreed with Jessica.

Gabriella snickered and replied, "Their resources are limited. Do not let your heart grow faint. Soon you will be going home." Those behind began to quicken their steps as they seemed to climb endlessly.

The door at the top of the staircase was unguarded and emptied into another lonely hallway. Gabriella stopped the group and stated, "We must be quiet from here on. We will be walking through enemy territory, and while your authority exceeds theirs, because of their numbers, it will be easier if we don't have to confront them." Waving her arm she added, "Come on."

They walked quietly through the maze of hallways, always following the light of Gabriella's orb. Some of the walls had windows that looked onto various control rooms. One room seemed to be a communication station where lesser spirits monitored phones. There they sent out or received reports that kept others along the chain of command informed and passed on orders. They spoke of defense against the plans of the King, but they seemed unaware of the group in the observation deck above them. The dark creatures' biggest accomplishment was hindering the King's people from their communication and following his orders. Daniel remembered what the Dragon had said about those who chose not to believe in the existence of this dimension and the existence of evil influences. Gabriella signaled again for the group to continue quietly. Daniel and the others followed.

As they turned a corner in the tunnel, Daniel stopped abruptly, causing each person behind him to run into the person in front of them, one after the other. "What is it?" came a whisper behind him.

"Look!" he whispered in response. The side of the wall gave way to a window that looked out on the landscape around the enemy base. The ground outside the window was gray and dead, pitted with large dimples and holes, the result of countless impact craters that were everywhere.

"Everyone thinks these are from asteroids hitting the base, but they are really battle scars." Everyone turned to look at Gabriella who pointed at the landscape before them. "Now look at the skyline, and tell me what you see." She pointed out the window.

Jessica drew in her breath and pointed above the dark, black horizon. "Look! Is that Earth? Are we on the Moon?"

"Yes," Gabriella whispered. "Now move forward quickly. The door home is on the other side of the control room. Come and see how they copy the work of the Kingdom unsuccessfully. Go quietly. Life is always easier if we are not being harassed by the enemy."

As the small contingent moved down the hallway, a large

room came into view where the Moon's surface had been. It reminded Daniel of images he had seen of mission control in Houston when the race to the moon had just started. In fact, the equipment looked from about the same time. "They really don't have all the neat equipment, do they?" Daniel whispered.

Gabriella responded, "They have copied that too. They are not creative like you. They are only thieves." Deformed alien creatures sat at consoles that displayed various news programs. Some consoles seemed to be watching individuals. Most were wealthy people who had video cameras all around them. "They think those cameras protect them, but they really just make it easier for the enemy to watch them," Gabriella said.

Daniel overheard one hissing creature speak into a microphone. "Tell him he is-s-s fat and ugly and that his-s-s-s wife is cheating on him-m-m." The creature made a hissing sound that might have sounded like a laugh. A similarly distorted laugh came from the headpiece that didn't quite fit the creature's head. The man on the screen looked in the mirror at himself and frowned deeply. He looked at the woman in the room with him, and contempt filled his eyes. Daniel wondered how many times this very thing had happened to others.

As they reached the other side, a door presented itself to the group. "Hurry! Come through. It will take you somewhere safe," Gabriella whispered. Daniel watched each person disappear as they went through the door. "Are you ready?" Gabriella asked Daniel. She extended her hand, and Daniel took it. Then they stepped through the door together.

CHAPTER 22

Onward

When Daniel and Gabriella appeared in the doorway portal, Daniel found himself in a lush garden with a stream and beautiful, tall trees. Just beyond the garden was a crystal-blue sea. The water was calm and peaceful. Daniel stopped to take in the beauty around him. The rest of the group walked ahead of him to tables covered with food.

The King stood behind Daniel and rested his hand on Daniel's shoulder. The King was no longer dressed in his glistening armor but was wearing a white robe and a blue sash. The King leaned close to whisper in Daniel's ear. "I want to show you something." He directed Daniel to look to his left where a portal had opened, revealing a soft, billowy cloud. It dissipated to reveal bright, white steps changing to a deep turquoise. Flames seemed to jump within them.

As Daniel and the King climbed the steps, Daniel felt a sensation envelop him that he didn't recognize. The King continued to climb the steps and couldn't seem to stop smiling.

As Daniel got closer, he was able to make out a white throne and a figure sitting on it. The King spoke. "Daniel, meet my Father and now your Father. Meet Love." Immediately, Daniel realized the sensation he was feeling was like waves of warm hugs as he had never felt before. Tears began to run down his cheeks.

When Daniel returned to the group, everyone was talking and comparing notes. Gabriella was explaining about their armor and the journey home.

Caleb had also joined the group. Daniel went to Caleb and hugged him. "You came back," Daniel exclaimed.

"Yeah," Caleb replied. "The King asked if I would help you kids get home. You will have to pass through some difficult territory, and he wanted me to guide you through it." Caleb smiled and patted Daniel on the back. "It feels good to be back in the battle and help others find their way."

Daniel smiled, nodded, and replied, "Glad you're here."

The King, Daniel, and Caleb joined the others at the table. Gabriella began the discussion. "It is time for you to make your journey home; however, you must travel through dangerous territory to get there."

At that point, the King spoke. "Remember, I am always with you." The group questioned how the King could be with them. Then, placing his hand on Daniel's chest, the King said, "I am here with each of you and in each of you." Then he smiled and patted Daniel's chest once again.

Sophia said, "Don't beat yourself up. That is the Darkness. Remind yourself of the words of the King. Encourage yourself and each other."

Gabriella added, "Those in the command center of the Darkness were complacent. They did not believe they were in any danger. Their ground forces are now aware of their potential for loss. Although the King has made claim and won the war, they continue to take down as many of the creative creatures as they can. They hate the final creature as much as they hate themselves. You must always be on guard." Gabriella took a deep breath. "Soon the King will send you into the fray. Go in the King's strength and power with peace. Go in love." Gabriella stepped back and vanished along with all the creatures who had come to send them off.

All those who remained activated their armor and prepared for the coming battle and the portal that would lead them to it. Before them appeared a rusty, iron gate decorated with swirling iron vines. Timothy whispered to Daniel, "It looks like the proverbial gates of hell."

Jessica, standing nearby, added, "How badly do we want to go home?" Each of them pondered their own reasons for going home. Daniel thought of his mother and wanted her to feel peace. Jessica thought of her father and her ill mother. Alex thought about how he would tell his aunt and uncle that he believed them. Samantha was unsure what she would say to her father. Justin wished his mother could see and believe the truths he had seen. Caleb thought of his little girls. With each of these considerations, they were all filled with resolve to complete their journeys.

When everyone was ready, Caleb reached for the handles on the gate and opened it. Suddenly, they were all sucked into a vortex of light and colors.

THE END

Follow Daniel and his friends as they journey through the lair of the Dragon and his kingdom of Darkness. There they will learn to use the King's power and bring the kingdom of Light home with them.

Acknowledgments

Thank you to my family and friends who gave me encouragement when I didn't believe in myself. I especially thank my two Carols—my sister, Carole Venters, who read and reread my manuscript from a reader's point of view and reluctantly and honestly provided advice and unveiled encouragement; and Carol Baird, my "comma queen," the first with advice and encouragement. I am also grateful for John Cochran and the team at Lucid Books for holding my hand through this first book. Finally, I want to thank that blue light within that guided and assisted me along the way. And thank you, the reader, for taking the time to go on this adventure with Daniel and his friends. May the ruler of this and the Quantum Realm speak to you too.

www.ingramcontent.com/pod-product-compliance
Lightning Source LLC
Chambersburg PA
CBHW070148100426
42743CB00013B/2850